DESIGNS
FOR
CASTLES
AND
COUNTRY VILLAS
BY
ROBERT & JAMES ADAM

DESIGNS

FOR
CASTLES
AND
COUNTRY VILLAS

BY

ROBERT & JAMES ADAM

Alistair Rowan

PHAIDON · OXFORD

The publisher acknowledges subsidy from the Scottish Arts Council towards the publication of this volume.

Phaidon Press Limited, Littlegate House, St Ebbe's Street, Oxford, OX1 1SQ

First published 1985
©Phaidon Press Limited 1985

British Library Cataloguing in Publication Data

Adam, Robert
   Designs for castles and country villas.
   1. Adam, Robert   2. Adam, James
   I. Title   II. Adam, James   III. Rowan, Alistair
   720'.92'2   NA997.A4

ISBN 0-7148-2278-7

Filmset and printed in Great Britain by BAS Printers Limited, Over Wallop, Hampshire

Contents

Preface

The designs for villas and country houses brought together in this book are probably not of a type that most people would readily associate with the name of Robert Adam. The Adam style is generally understood to mean something else. It has to do with richness of effect, with fineness and with opulent elaboration. It is moreover a style that has, or appears to have, essential links with the art of interior decoration, so that to talk of an Adam chimney-piece, or an Adam ceiling, conveys an immediate, clear impression, whereas such phrases as an Adam plan or an Adam façade do not. Decoration is certainly an element in the art of architecture and one in which the Adam brothers worked with unique brilliance, yet it may be questioned whether Robert, or his partner James, would have been content that their legacy to the stock of British historic architecture should be assessed now, as it so often is, primarily in decorative terms. The Adam style is more varied and the personality of the brothers more robust.

In historical terms it might be argued that the Adams have become the victims of their industry and success. The energy of Robert Adam was astonishing. A catalogue of more than 180 individual commissions carried into execution and almost 9,000 architectural drawings in the Soane Museum bear witness to an artist, and to an organizer, of prodigious capacity; yet a man who achieves so much, and for whose activities so many records remain, runs the risk of being never fully understood. For two decades from 1758, the brothers stood at the peak of their profession. From 1773, as a record of their success, they issued the well-known plates of *The Works in Architecture of Robert and James Adam*, a collection of the most prestigious designs, serving to keep their name before the public and to disseminate the Adam style. The published *Works* however have had a secondary effect, as to many architectural historians the commissions recorded there have become *the* Adam style. It is not surprising that analysis should often be concentrated on these busy years which count most in terms of the brothers' impact on European taste—the very

existence of the book determined such a focus—yet Robert and James had almost twenty years of joint practice still before them when the *Works* first appeared.

It is my hope that this volume, issued some two hundred years after its first conception, may act as an introduction to the Adams' late style and that, in limiting its contents to what may reasonably be supposed to have found a place in the pattern book which the Adams planned but did not publish, a representative selection of their later domestic architecture has been made. One advantage which an eighteenth-century pattern book enjoys over a modern architectural monograph is the much greater number of plans which it contains. The buildings illustrated here are, in the majority of cases, very fully described, which I believe will be useful in a book that aims to break new ground. There can in any case be little doubt that this manner of publishing their late work is one which the brothers themselves had already chosen.

The existence of this volume has been made possible first through the kind co-operation of the Trustees of Sir John Soane's Museum, who have permitted the Adam drawings to be reproduced, and second through the enthusiasm of my publishers, ever ready with encouragement for what may at times have seemed either an over-academic—or even an over-imaginative—approach to the architectural historian's role. To both I am most grateful. I should like also to record my particular thanks to Sir John Summerson, Miss Dorothy Stroud and Miss Christine Scull who each assisted me in my work at the museum; and to Mr. Mark Ritchie, Miss Penelope Marcus and Miss Barbara Mercer of Phaidon Press who, at different times and with great patience, have helped with their expertise. I am also grateful to Mr. Horst Kolo who not only took the photographs of the drawings reproduced here but also provided me with extra prints from which I have prepared the modern drawings needed to make good the gaps amongst the original designs.

Research for this volume would not have been possible

without the kind co-operation of Mr. Keith Adam of Blair Adam, Sir John Clerk of Penicuik, Bart., and Professor David C. Simpson of the University of Edinburgh, each of whom permitted me to consult papers in their possession relating to the Adam family or to the brothers' practice. In sifting through this documentary material I have been particularly helped by Dr. Margaret H. B. Sanderson of the Scottish Record Office whose knowledge of the detail of Robert and James Adam's last years has been invaluable. I have received much kindness from the staff of the National Monuments Records in England and in Scotland, particularly from Miss Kitty Cruft and Mr. Ian Gow who helped to identify a number of possible sites and clients, from the British Architectural Library, the Library of Trinity College Dublin, the Institute of Historical Research in the University of London; Drummond's Bank and from the R.I.B.A. Drawings Collection. I have also been helped with various specific enquiries by Mr. Marcus Binney, Mr. Howard Colvin, Mr. John Harris, Mr. David Learmont, Dr. Edward McParland, Dr. David Rainsford Hannay, the Earl and Countess of Rosebery, the Rev. Jeremy Saville, Professor Alan A. Tait and Mr. and Mrs. Fred Walker of Wyreside.

In conclusion I must thank Mrs. Blathnait Crowley, who has typed a complex manuscript with promptness and precision, my mother-in-law, Mrs. Charles Wrinch, who for two summers has surrendered her attic to academic pursuits, and finally my wife, Ann Martha, whose careful attention to detail and scrupulous regard for the written word is such a comfort in the final throes of bringing a book to birth.

Alistair Rowan

DUBLIN, November 1984

Introduction

The book that is assembled here starts with many dis- advantages: it has no text nor even a title, while the documentary proof that it ever existed in the minds of its creators rests on one single reference in a letter of an employee. The contents have had to be determined by a succession of suppositions or deductions, and yet, when all is said, the value of the work must rest secure in the repu- tation of its would-be authors, Robert and James Adam, two of the most noted architects of eighteenth-century Europe. When in 1822 the third and last volume of *The Works in Architecture of Robert and James Adam* was published posthumously in London, the world of British architecture believed, as it has continued to do, that the brothers' final contribution to the stock of European pattern books was made. Only one man, John Paterson, once the principal clerk of their Edinburgh office, and possibly a middle-aged · draughtsman or two, realized that the nucleus of an alto- gether different book of Adam designs had once been in existence. Part of it survived among the brothers' collected drawings, then in the possession of their niece, Susan Clerk, and soon to be bought by John Soane for safekeeping in his London home at No. 12 Lincoln's Inn Fields. It is these drawings now in Sir John Soane's Museum, that provide the principal evidence for the existence of a project for a further architectural publication by Robert and James Adam, a work to be devoted to their designs for modest classical villas or for houses in what they called the castle style. Though the origins of the book lie in the 1780s, draw- ings were still being prepared for it when Robert died in 1792 and even to within a few months of James's death in October 1794; we must therefore assume that it was the deaths of both men rather than a loss of impetus that consigned this final foray into architectural publication to the realms of what might have been. Had James lived, the book would probably have been published and, though it is pointless now to speculate on what influence on British architecture it might or might not have had, there can be little doubt that the range of the brothers' achievement would have been more widely understood had it appeared; that some of their smaller houses which have been lost would have survived; and that we would have had, in the accompanying letterpress, an authoritative exposition of what has troubled many an architectural critic, the mean- ing of the Adam castle style. Of one thing we may be sure: this last volume of the brothers' work displays a very dif- ferent sort of architecture to the opulent classicism and profuse interior display that is, for many, synonymous with the name of Robert Adam. Their final book was not to be a stylish rearrangement of already well-worked themes: its architecture was new.

THE PUBLICATIONS OF THE ADAM FAMILY

That Robert and James Adam should turn their thoughts to a publication on their smaller villas in later life is entirely in character with their practice. Publication, or at least the intention to publish, runs like the theme of a rondo through both their lives. William Adam, their father and founder of the family fortune, began the process with the prospectus of his *Vitruvius Scoticus* in 1727. The book was begun, carried so far and then laid aside to be modernized and augmented by the eldest son John, who in turn left the work incomplete so that it was not published until 1812 and then merely as a collection of plates without any text.[1] While filial piety prompted John to attempt to finish his father's volume, Robert—determined to play a part in an altogether larger theatre—declared that the great collec- tion of engravings of Roman antiquities by Antoine Desgodetz, *Les Edifices Antiques de Rome* of 1682, was quite inaccurate. In 1754 he wrote from Italy proposing that a new corrected edition should be published in English. He engaged draughtsmen in Rome. Buildings were measured, plates prepared by Piranesi, and a text begun, yet once again the promises of publication proved illusory.

No Adam edition of Desgodetz exists and the plates are now lost. About the same time Robert prepared a set of *Designs for Vases and Foliage Composed from the Antique* for which copper plates were made; these too were left unpublished and only appeared in 1822, long after his death. The work that stands as a monument to Adam industry abroad is thus neither Desgodetz nor the *Designs for Vases* but *The Ruins of the Palace of the Emperor Diocletian at Spalatro*, a site that Robert had surveyed in the summer of 1757 shortly before he returned to London at the end of his grand tour. This erudite and sumptuous folio volume with plates engraved in Venice, was published in London in 1764, by which time the Adam revolution in interior design was well under way and Robert had already enjoyed the prestige that publication can bring, albeit vicariously, in the dedication to himself of Piranesi's *Il Campo Marzio dell'Antica Roma* of 1762.[2]

While the book on Diocletian's Palace and the Desgodetz project were intended to secure a place for Adam amongst the *literati* of his day, as an architect he was no less conscious of the contribution that publication might make to the furtherance of his own career. Some of Robert's earliest commissions seem to have been issued first as single engraved sheets: the Admiralty screen in Whitehall in February 1761, the screen walls to Carlton House and Shelburne House in 1767, and the perspective view of the brothers' Adelphi development which was begun in July 1768. Appearing in 1770, the self-congratulatory caption for this last plate offers clear proof that the brothers were well aware of the propaganda value inherent in architectural publications.[3] In much the same spirit the Adams were to send drawings to John Woolfe and James Gandon for their continuation of *Vitruvius Britannicus* in 1767 and 1771.[4] Two years later the first part of the first volume of their *Works in Architecture* was issued, a series which within the brothers' lifetimes was to extend to two folio volumes each made up of five parts published intermittently between 1773 and 1779.[5] At one stage in his career James, who had a penchant for theoretical argument, and who contibuted the prefaces to *The Works*, began a 'Treatise on Architecture', which he left incomplete;[6] then, to the general surprise of his family and friends, he brought out in 1789 *Practical Essays on Agriculture*, a subject on which, as the proprietor of a *ferme ornée* in Hertfordshire, he could claim to have a little personal knowledge.[7]

Against such a background of prospectuses and publications the proposition that Robert and James intended to produce one final book of their latest designs will perhaps not seem unreasonable. It might be argued that they would have done better to see through the press the final folio volume of *The Works in Architecture* but against this two points may be made. First, it would not, on existing evidence, be out of character for the architects to abandon one project when another seemed more attractive or more likely to succeed and, second, there is no evidence beyond the assertion of the publishers, Priestley and Weale of Bloomsbury, that the ill-assorted assemblage of views and half-completed plates in their third volume was ever intended by the Adams to be placed before the public.

Several of the plates had been published individually as single issues at an earlier date, three more are clearly prepared as part of the appeal literature for the new college for the University of Edinburgh, while others showing details present the scantiest of visual images, lacking entirely the richness of composition that distinguishes the pages of the first two volumes, and lacking, significantly, any explanatory captions or even a date of publication. Rather than disproving the possibility of an intended final book of late designs the very imperfect and incomplete state of the posthumous volume of *The Works* seems to support the proposal.[8] By 1786 when a second printing of the second volume of *The Works* was issued, the Adams' attention as publishers was already engaged elsewhere. By then they were planning a different type of book to present a different sort of building and had no interest in collecting fresh material for further issues of *The Works*.

THE EVIDENCE OF THE ADAM DRAWINGS

Evidence of the intention of the Adam brothers to publish a book of later designs is supplied by some sets of plans and elevations, preserved among the volumes of Adam drawings now in the Soane Museum. Though some of these volumes, notably those that contain original sketches by Robert, can be shown to have been begun by the architect himself, most of the volumes must have been made up several years after both the brothers had died, probably by William Adam, the last surviving brother, by his sister Margaret and by his niece, Susan Clerk.

At the time that the practice was wound up there were two Adam offices, one at 13 Albemarle Street, London and the other in Edinburgh. The Adams were always described as being a loving and closely-knit family, and indeed the domestic arrangements of the brothers bear this out, for their sisters played a considerable and a continuous role in their lives: two spinsters, Elizabeth and Margaret, looked after Robert and James in London and, when Robert travelled north to attend to the Scottish practice, two married sisters, Susan, the wife of John Clerk of Eldin, and Mary, married to the Rev. Dr. John Drysdale, minister of the Tron church, Edinburgh, attended to his needs. After Mrs. Drysdale had been left a widow Robert was to employ her as a type of family overseer in the Edinburgh office, moving her to a large house at 14 Nicolson Street where his draughtsmen and his principal clerk, John Paterson—later succeeded by Hugh Cairncross—all worked. In Edinburgh Mrs. Drysdale was to prove fiercely protective of her brother's reputation and of his interests.[9]

With James's death in London in 1794 the Adam practice came abruptly to an end. William, predominantly a businessman and builders' merchant was left to look after his spinster sisters, helped by his niece Susan Clerk, the daughter of Mr. and Mrs. John Clerk of Eldin, who came down from Edinburgh to London about 1795 and by 1810 was settled permanently in the Adam household. Susan Clerk, as William's sole heir, inherited the Adam drawings which she sold for £200 to Sir John Soane in 1833.[10]

There is no conclusive evidence as to who compiled the individual volumes of drawings or when they were made up, but we do have a date for the uniting of the Edinburgh office collection with the main holding in the Albemarle Street house. In the autumn of 1796 Mrs. Drysdale, who had become anxious about the safety of the drawings in her care, sent them down to London. A letter to Peggy Adam, postmarked 19 December that year, makes this clear and also suggests that it was she and Susan Clerk who were expected to sort the drawings:

I wonder if you and Susy are begun to the task of getting all the drawings put in order? I dare say it will be a very laborious one. I was sorry when Mr. and Mrs. Clerk told me that you was mad at the Box with the drawings being sent from ther[sic]. You had never said anything positively against it and I did not consider them as at all safe in this place. There was not a single place in the world either in the Box or out of it without running the risk of being destroyed by damp and I was quite unhappy at their being at the mercy of anybody that chused to go into Cairncrosses house when he was out of it and break open the box and take out any drawings they pleased. I always had a dread of that fellow Patterson playing some mischief and was glad when I got them away.[11]

The drawings which were brought into one collection by December 1796 fell into three categories: sketches and ideal plans, which the brothers seem to have used as a reservoir of ideas; the picturesque landscapes of classical and romantic subject matter that Robert drew by way of diversion; and those drawings that related directly to the Adams' practice as architects. Many of the sketches had been bound into small folio volumes during the brothers' lifetimes while Robert had apparently kept his watercolours carefully numbered in sets and arranged in special albums.[12] All the office drawings—by far the largest group—were loose and, as Mary Drysdale foresaw, to put them in order must have been a laborious and problematical business. What was to be kept and what could be thrown out? Were some drawings complete in themselves or part of a larger set divided between the two offices? And, given the decision to store them in bound volumes, how best could they all be arranged? While the office was a going concern the drawings for various commissions had been kept in rolls, identified with a brief inscription on the outside edge, and stored in open shelves or racks. Many went back to the early 1760s and, as dirt marks still prove, were covered in dust. All will have had that irritating tendency to roll themselves up again the instant they were left free. The size varied; some would have to be folded perhaps two or three times before they would fit into a volume while others were so small as to require a separate backing sheet. Certainly the work of collation and cross-reference will have been both tedious and grimy, and Peggy Adam's exasperation with her sister at sending down the contents of the Edinburgh office unannounced is not hard to understand.

The Adams in London wasted little time considering what might be thrown out. Much the easiest decision was to keep everything: scraps and doodles, pencil memoranda of the sort that a busy man writes to himself, scribbled plans with calculations of the price of a job, rough office outlines pricked through and only half completed, as well as the regular plans, sections, elevations and interior designs standard to any architect's office.

It has sometimes been said that the work of sorting these drawings destroyed the original sequence of the Adams' arrangement and that Susan Clerk and her uncle William, on whom the burden of reorganization seems principally to have fallen, set aside a logical and coherent system of arrangement in preference for a fancy scheme of their own.[13] This view is not supported by the very random survival of drawings from different dates and schemes, where some structures are almost completely described while others are represented only by one or two drawings, and it is against experience to suggest that all the drawings of a practice that had lasted nearly forty years—sketches, designs, copies and details—should have survived intact in an unaltered sequence. The Adam drawings, like any large collection of papers, posed serious problems: if in some places they had a certain coherence, in others they were in a mess. Mrs. Drysdale's anxiety to prevent Paterson from helping himself and Robert's warnings to the staff in Edinburgh not to let drawings get into other hands suggest that pilfering took place and that the check which the offices could keep on old material was at best imperfect.[14]

The Soane Museum collection of Adam drawings numbers a total of 8,641 sheets stuck into 55 volumes, mostly of a large folio size. To give some sense of order to this vast body of material the drawings must first have been sorted into different piles bringing similar subjects together. Thus a basic distinction was made in the arrangement of the volumes between sketches and finished drawings while individual volumes, in either category, were devoted to single subject types—ceiling designs, chimney-pieces, mirrors, furniture—or to more architectural subjects such as the plans for entire buildings. Where possible a distinction was made between designs that were prepared for the country or for town, and between public and private works, though the building designs for a particular client were often grouped in one volume.

It is the designs for buildings that concern us here and fortunately we know a little more about how these volumes were prepared. Among the family papers from Blair Adam two handlists, drawn up about 1818, index the drawings in 23 of the Adam volumes.[15] The lists are not always complete and it is hard to tell whether they were drawn up as an aid to compiling the volumes or, as seems more likely, as a guide to what they contained. These lists appear to be written partly by William Adam and partly by Susan Clerk. Each entry names a client or a commission, followed first by the number of the volume in which the drawings appear, then by an 'article' number which indicates their position in the volume, and finally the exact number of sheets or 'pieces' that are contained in each article. From the arrangement of the lists it seems that the volumes that contain the brothers' designs for buildings were compiled first by collecting together in one 'article' all the drawings for a particular commission and then by combining sets of all these collected sheets to make up a book of between 60 or 100 pages. Many of the drawings in the volumes are inscribed on the back with notes such as 'This should go third into the book', or 'These plans go 21st into Book 5', though the placing proposed does not always match the sequence of the drawings today.[16] With some 'articles' the compilers appear to have made several attempts to contrive a satisfactory order; elsewhere uncle and niece abandon all hope of a system and the volume is assembled simply by transferring several rolls of drawings directly into its pages!

Amongst the volumes, one, numbered 20 in the Adam index, now no. 46, differs from the rest in a number of ways. In the first place the type of drawing is unusual for, though some sheets could possibly have been prepared in the normal course of business, many more show plans and elevations neatly related together on one page which is a layout not normally found in Adam work. Most are highly finished with carefully graded monochrome washes on the elevations, and their scale, generally, is smaller than that used by the brothers for routine office work. Some are

drawn to an almost miniature size which permits a total of 60 different schemes to be represented—some very fully—in the first 78 pages of the volume. All the buildings shown are houses. Susan Clerk, or whoever was responsible for arranging this particular volume, seems to have identified these drawings as in some sense special. As if in response to the neatness of the drawings, the pages have been laid out in as orderly a way as possible (Fig. 1). Some of the drawings are rough enough, it is true, but in several places the sheets are arranged to form a symmetrical pattern and at times one pattern has been tried out and then altered to another. Though the individual size of sheets and the type of draughtsmanship may vary, there is a degree of care and deliberation in the makeup of the volume which is not found in the other books of Adam building plans. Most of the drawings are bordered by a black line and in some cases these have clearly been added to reinforce, if in an amateurish way, the impression of the book as a single unit.

When volume 46 was compiled, very few of the drawings were identified or carried any inscription. At some stage

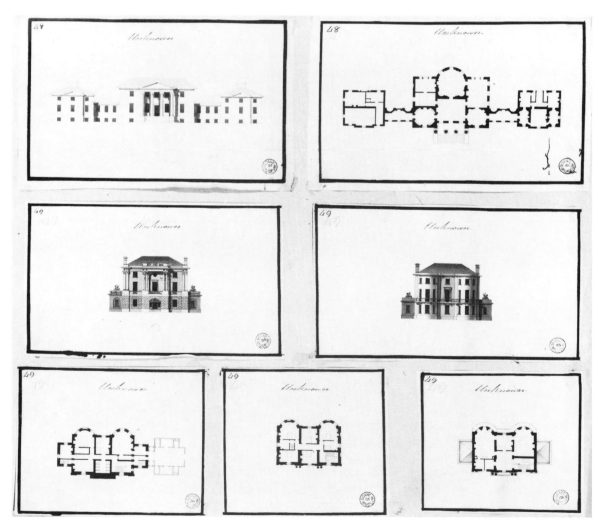

Fig. 1. Seven small-scale drawings from page 61 of volume 46 of the Adam drawings in Sir John Soane's Museum. The two designs at the top are for Cadland and the lower set is for Rosebank. The broad ink borders have been added by the compilers of the Adam volumes. Faint pencil borders which may be seen in the drawings for Cadland may represent the intended size for the engraver's plate.

somebody with a little knowledge of the work that had been passing through the office—probably William Adam or perhaps an older clerk—went through the piles of drawings noting where he could the names of buildings, or adding those of clients, to such sheets which, in the process of undoing the brothers' rolls of plans, had been rendered anonymous. Whoever did this work often remembered wrongly, so that inscriptions on the Adam drawings today cannot always be taken as accurate.[17] Sometimes the identifications were written in pencil to be overwritten more carefully in ink; in other cases a scribbled addition in pen extends what was clearly an office inscription. In the case of volume 46, each separate building was given a number corresponding to the 'article' number in William Adam's and Susan Clerk's index. Some were further identified, usually by the name of the client, while many more were marked 'unknown'.

The internal evidence of these drawings—the neatness of their presentation, their unusual scale, the fact that they originally bore no inscription and the standardization of their general appearance—strongly suggests that they were prepared for the use of an engraver and that what is preserved in volume 46 of the Adam drawings is a considerable number of the drawings for the plates of a projected publication of the brothers' late works. The lack of any inscription particularly points to this, as the drawings would have been prepared first for an artists' engraver who would have produced a set of plates of the drawings alone, a state known to the trade as 'before letters' and one that is conveniently demonstrated within the Adams' own practice by the incomplete engravings, without any inscription, that make up many of the plates in the spurious third volume of *The Works*. The neat and didactic layout of some individual sheets of drawings supports the same view: indeed the preparation of pages such as those for Tullysoul, Jervistown House and Captain Pitts's villa (Pls. 1, 6 and 7) cannot be satisfactorily explained as routine office production in the practice of two busy architects.

One piece of evidence tends to confirm the supposition that these drawings came into being as the plates of a book. This is contained in a letter from John Paterson, Adam's chief clerk in the Edinburgh office, who subsequently incurred Mrs. Drysdale's disapproval by leaving in 1791 to set up on his own. Writing to Robert Adam on 8 February 1790, Paterson reports on progress at the university buildings, on the work of the mason James Crichton and on his son Richard who had been employed as a draughtsman in the Adam Edinburgh office. He then adds a notice on office business, very much as an aside, though it is vital to the present argument: 'I have got a young man to assist me in forwarding the Book and I have treyed [trained] him to draw and he copey very well so I have no use for Crichton'.[18] As many of the designs recorded in volume 46 prove to have been made for Scottish clients, it seems probable that these small-scale copy drawings were prepared in Edinburgh in the spring of 1790 either by Richard Crichton or by his young successor, possibly John Charels whom Paterson mentions in a letter later that year. Considering the miniature scale that the drawings adopt, the eyesight of 'a young man' is exactly what was required.

THE CONTENTS OF THE VOLUME

If the brothers' intention to publish a book of their later designs can be established beyond reasonable doubt, the contents of the volume remain less certain. The evidence of the designs prepared for an engraver and preserved in volume 46 is confusing and suggests in the first place that the brothers for some time were uncertain as to the best scale to adopt for their designs. Eighteenth-century architects' publications do not of course conform to any set scale from one design to another; nor even within the one design or page is the scale necessarily the same. None the less there is usually a convention whereby schemes occupy approximately the same space within the engraved page, whatever the variations in scale from one design to another. In an age that preceded the use of a standard rule marked with different scales, the architect's dividers were his most essential tool, hence their frequent use in portraiture to indicate an architectural calling. With dividers universally employed, a drawn scale was all that was required to indicate a change in ratio from page to page, though for obvious reasons the scale of a plan, elevation and section tended to remain the same within one design. The Adam brothers' drawings for their volume of villa and castle designs exist in two quite distinct visual scales: a large scale of about 1 inch to 12 feet, and a smaller scale, 'miniature' in character, which is usually about 1 inch to 25 feet. It seems unlikely that the large- and miniature-scale designs were intended to be used as illustrations in the same book: the visual 'jump' would have been disconcerting with façades of say 60 feet in length appearing on one page as no more than $2\frac{1}{4}$ inches and elsewhere as a full 5 inches in width. There is no precedent in eighteenth-century British architectural publications for variations of this degree; moreover, the disparity of page size, generally about 14 to 16 by 9 inches for the large designs and, though more variable, about 5 by 9 or 11 inches for the miniature plans, makes it improbable that they could have formed part of the same volume. There is moreover an interim scale between the larger and the miniature designs, though used for only one set of drawings, which suggests that the brothers, or their clerks, for some time kept an open mind on the shape and size of the book they were to produce.

Of the schemes for the book that have been preserved, most are drawn to the miniature scale. Twenty-one exist at this size while a possible total of nine more are recorded in larger-scale drawings.[19] Twice houses, which appear among larger-scale drawings—Brasted Place and Sunnyside (Pls. 8 and 28)—reappear as miniature designs; otherwise the buildings recorded to the two scales are different. The two houses, existing in both scales probably indicate that at some stage the format of the book was fixed and a decision was made to reduce all the designs to approximately the same size while the balance of the evidence, both in the preponderance of the miniature drawings and in the uniformity of their appearance, suggests that the book was to have been published to the smaller scale.

It is also likely that at the time of the brothers' deaths a considerably larger number of the miniature plans had been prepared than now exists. This is suggested by the arrangement of the drawings in volume 46, which contains five completely blank folio pages between miniature designs for classical houses and miniature drawings of castle-style schemes, with two further blank pages at the end of the castles, after which very large scale drawings of rustic cottages and lodges make up the rest of the volume. Though the Adam drawings have suffered notable losses by theft, these seven blank pages never had any designs on them. They were left blank intentionally, as if Susan Clerk, while compiling the volumes, was aware of the existence somewhere of more miniature plans that might have completed the set—plans which in the event either never turned up or were not stuck into the volume.

That many miniature designs were missing by the time Susan Clerk set to work is evident from the range of drawings that survives. Thus in some cases minor commissions, which were not to be built, are very fully described— Beckenham Rectory (Pl. 22) is a case in point—while an important house like Culzean Castle is represented only by two small (and partial) floor plans. It must be assumed that when the drawings were first made a commission such as Culzean would have been given as much prominence as the smaller scheme. Certainly it could not have been published on the basis of the ground and first floor plans alone, so we may conclude that more drawings of elevations, sections and plans of Culzean and of many other houses were prepared to the miniature scale and have since been lost. To these presumed losses must be added thirteen drawings which have been removed from the pages of miniature designs. What these designs were can be deduced in many cases from their position in the volume. Thus Brasted Place and High Down, Airthrey and Dalquharran are all houses for which some miniature designs have demonstrably been lost. The buildings shown on six other drawings removed from pages 55 and 57 cannot now be known.

Though volume 46 is the primary source from which the putative contents of the brothers' publication may be reconstructed, it is not the sole source of drawings that appear to have been prepared for publication. Other miniature plans, identical in scale with drawings in volume 46, exist among the sketch designs in volume 1, from which three further Scottish castles—Bewley, Findlater, and what may be a design for Stevenson of Braidwood—can be added to the probable contents of the book. We are left then with a total of twenty-four houses for which some miniature plans exist, to which may be added eight or nine other designs drawn to the larger scale. The total number of houses intended to be published in the book is thus not less than thirty-two and could well have been greater.

Besides these drawings there is no clear evidence on the number of buildings that the brothers planned to publish in their book. To judge from the Blair Adam index, four extra 'unknown' houses were once represented by miniature drawings now missing from volume 46[20] and the possibility that several more designs were drawn up for publication cannot be ruled out. If drawings did once exist for all the seven pages left blank by the compilers the total number of buildings or designs to be included in the book

could reasonably be advanced to as many as fifty.

So far as we can tell, none of the drawings prepared for this book was ever engraved. The surviving designs are all neat and clean with no trace of the over-scoring, the drafting of diagonals to establish centres or the application of an emulsion on the back which will often indicate when an eighteenth-century drawing has been to a plate-maker's shop.[21] Nor is there any hint in the publicity produced by Priestley and Weale, who bought the remainder of the brothers' engraved work in the Adam sale of 1821, that they had acquired any material relevant to this final publication.[22] Without the plates the size of the book must remain an open question. Even so the scale of the drawings seems to indicate a more modest publication than the folios on Diocletian's palace or *The Works* whose generous scale was intended to attract rich clients and to carry the name of Robert Adam into the houses of the aristocracy. By the 1780s minor clients, for whom Robert might have had less time in the 1760s and 1770s, now played a significant role in generating work for the office. City merchants and professional men, members of the Church, the services or of the House of Commons, country gentlemen or representatives of the provincial and Scottish nobility, these were the people on whom the Adams' practice now depended and for whom the new book was planned. Comparatively minor architects like John Crunden and Thomas Rawlins had had considerable success with straightforward books of this sort, unpretentious practitioners whose proposals might match a gentleman's pocket as easily as their sensible quarto volumes fitted into his bookcase shelves.[23] Evidently the brothers identified the need for such an outlet for their own designs and by the late 1780s had set draughtsmen to work on the book.

DESIGN CONSIDERATIONS

The houses that appear in this volume divide formally into two groups: the classical designs and those buildings of a more romantic character which were to be called castles. Whether Robert Adam thought of his castles in quite such a separate way as we do today is a point to which we will have to return, but it is evident as far as exterior appearance is concerned that we are dealing here with two quite different sorts of architecture. The Adam castles are something radically new, apparently without precedent in Europe, while the classical houses fit into an established tradition. Occasionally, though not very often, the Adam drawings in the Soane Museum record commissions where the brothers offered alternative classical and castle-style schemes—two examples in this volume are Wyreside and Airthrey Castle[24]—yet on the whole the two styles do not, as in a set of nineteenth-century competition drawings, appear to compete with each other. The brothers might experiment with a number of variants for a villa or a castle and might, like other architects who published designs, treat the public to a display of their alternative proposals, yet when this happens the different proposals tend to be for buildings in the same genre. The larger schemes for

Brasted Place or for Kirkdale of which there are two extra elevations, are in each case patently the same building; while the many plans for Sunnyside grow one out of another.[25] In the same way Findlater Castle might be said to develop from the final version of Culzean which itself owes a great deal to Dalquharran or to a still earlier project, the second scheme for The Oaks. There is then a sort of internal consistency within the castles and classical houses, as if the brothers thought of the two styles as offering a fundamental choice, which once made and agreed with a client was not changed. What would be changed, and in some cases might pass through a bewildering sequence of alterations, would be the detail of a particular design. Adam lived in an age that had brought to perfection qualities of refinement and variation as cornerstones in the creative arts. If the decision to compose a design in a classical or in a castle style might be compared to the musician's choice of a major or a minor key, the architect's way of going about a design bears a striking similarity to that most popular musical form of his day, the theme and variations. Each project is to some extent a variation of an earlier design, a variation wrought with great brilliance and with such ease that it may seem to reject elements that were essential in its predecessor and yet remain linked to it. In these processes of development and transposition, variety and refinement are the ends that Adam always has in view, while his fundamental theme resides in the purity and the potential for perfection of geometry.

That Adam was fascinated by geometry is evident from many of these designs. Some, like the astonishing scheme for Barnbougle Castle, owe an obvious debt to Italy and to that virtuoso pattern-making which, in the Papal and French academies, had largely replaced real planning in the prize projects.[26] In his twenties Adam had found such exercises infectious and, though he was never to achieve in reality the concatenation of chambers or sequences of axially ordered perspectives that such visions involved, the potential of a geometrically ordered structure would remain in his mind all his life. It was in Rome, in the projects for the various *concorsi* and in the archaeological reconstructions of Piranesi, that Adam first encountered an architecture that depended on the intersection of a number of axes, meeting usually in angles of 45 degrees, and culminating in an heroic central space on an oval or circular plan.[27] Variety and novelty are implicit in such axial designs and Adam, who sought above all else to create effects of surprise in his plans, to catch even the most cultivated visitor by an unexpected shift of direction or modulation of space, systematically employs a variety of axes in many of the villa and castle designs. This geometrical play reaches its peak in schemes like Barnbougle, Great Saxham and Wyke Manor; it is present in the castle-style designs laid out on a V-shaped or a D-shaped plan; it appears in the triangular villa at Walkinshaw, the 'cloverleaf' plan for Sunnyside and with quite perfect ingenuity in Mr. Wilson's charming casino.

If such complex and intricate structures fit neatly into a pattern of advanced architectural theory in the later eighteenth century, there are other apparently simpler villas that match a different aspect of contemporary thought.

Geometry for Robert Adam may provide a visually rich interrelationship of spaces, a picturesque interior aesthetic strongly articulated by apses, niches and screens of columns, yet at its most fundamental the architect's respect for geometry appears not in the manipulation of space but in the mass of his exterior forms. It is evident from many of the schemes recorded in this volume that in the brothers' smaller designs a completely rational clarity dictated their choice of forms. Simple rectangular villas, with clearly articulated façades, rise as pure blocks of stone (Pls. 2, 3, 12 and 22) or are linked by straight corridors to square or rectangular wings (Pls. 7, 23, 29, 31 and 34). In their most simple form the effects of mass are heightened by the use of plain roofs, by centrally massed chimney stacks and by a masonry surface that is without decoration, except for an occasional string course, or the negative interruption of a window opening without an architrave. Here the architecture which is proposed is reduced to a minimum, yet it springs from Adam's awareness of the geometrical basis of his art no less than do the elaborate plans. If in the more complex schemes geometry provides the starting point for a spatial elaboration that becomes a *tour de force*, so too in the little classical villas it lies at the heart of an architectural style as understated as it is scrupulously controlled. What we encounter here is not a contradiction between simplicity and complexity but a coherent architecture which develops logically from a geometrical basis towards two different extremes.

A comparison between a villa designed for a Mr. Thomson (Pl. 3) and Mr. Wilson's casino (Pls. 14 and 15) may illustrate these extremes. Both are small houses between 45 and 50 feet wide and each proposes a hall, a staircase, two main reception rooms and a study (or a bedroom) on the main floor. Here however the similarities cease, for Mr. Thomson's villa is worked out largely in terms of plain rectangular rooms while the casino has one of the most intricate plans ever devised by Adam. No one would dispute the essentially geometrical content of this plan, the variety of shape that it achieves or the refinement with which it is developed. The end result seems so original as to suggest that it may be unique, yet if we refer to the concept of theme and variations as suggested above we may note that Mr. Wilson's casino is developed from a plan type that is essentially similar to the 'clover-leaf' villa project (Pls. 26 and 27) and is identical in its circulation pattern, though not in its appearance, to Sunnyside as it was built (Pl. 28). In elevation none of these projects has much in common yet each employs a set of motifs that Adam adopted and adapted from time to time in his designs. In the case of the casino it is one of the most heroic themes that is fused with this intricate plan; for the garden façade quotes the Bramante *tempietto*, albeit in a rustic, anglicized version. The colonnaded loggia that this provides has obvious links with the loggias on the bowed frontage of Great Saxham House (Pl. 13), with the garden front of Hill House, Putney (Pl. 18), or with the quadrant corners of Adam's university buildings in Edinburgh. In an inverted form we might even detect a thematic link with the great colonnaded staircases, lit by glass domes, that Adam proposed for several houses and ultimately built at Culzean. Thus, as is the case with the plan, the treatment of the elevations may be shown to bear thematic links with other examples of Adam's architecture. It is the effortless originality and freshness of invention in designs such as these that gives enduring interest to the brothers' later castle and villa schemes.

THE CLASSICAL VILLAS

The villas and castles included in this volume are likely to have been presented to the public, if Robert or James had written any text, as convenient and novel designs. In many ways they are, yet the novelty of the villas and of two at least of the larger classical houses is only comparative. Robert Adam is an architect who throughout his life drew his ideas from a wide variety of sources, refining and reshaping them in his mind before they were to re-emerge in a characteristically Adamesque way. His form of classicism, if highly polished and refined, is rooted firmly in the architectural traditions of the English eighteenth century. The clarity, already noted, of the juxtaposition of elements in the more straightforward villas derives from the preferences of English Palladianism, which also provides the source for the rusticated basement storeys, the clearly articulated ground floors and horizontal emphasis in many of the villas and even in the castle designs. In the case of the classical villas, the example of two Palladians, Roger and Robert Morris, seems to provide essential inspiration.

Roger Morris was personally known to the Adam family as the architect of Inveraray Castle in Argyll for which William Adam, and after 1748 John and Robert, had had responsibility as overseers.[28] At Marble Hill near Twickenham and at Combe Bank in Kent, where Robert was later to make additions, Morris had built early examples of the simply proportioned, understated villa, roofed with a single slate pyramid of a type that Adam was later to adapt in a number of his own designs. Roger Morris also acted as artistic mentor to the surveyor Robert Morris, an early advocate of austere and rational architecture, whose *Lectures on Architecture* were first read in London in 1734. The second volume of the lectures is dedicated to Roger Morris, who is credited with 'the ideas of the designs' which are discussed in the book, and the burden of Morris's theory— that beauty in architecture resides primarily in proportion and the well-ordering of the parts of a whole—is clearly demonstrated by the plans and elevations in the plates which are for simple, unembellished houses often with pyramid roofs. In his text Robert Morris reproves those architects who sacrifice the convenience and proper functioning of an interior to outward show, whose houses do not work as plans and who 'garnish the inelegant design to atone for the disproportion of the parts'.[29] His plans are based on rational concepts of order and utility, and a number of the elevations are of a simplicity to match the most straightforward of the Adam villas. We can well imagine the text which the brothers might have prepared for their book upholding similar standards of design. Another consideration which Morris is the first to explore, the influence of situation on the style of a design, is one that has immediate relevance to the Adam's villa and castle schemes. Architectural style for Morris is dictated by location: 'no building should be designed to be erected without first considering the extent of prospect, hills, vales etc. which expand or encircle it.' It is from these that the architect should take his ideas, and 'the modus must be shifted from one scene to another as necessity requires.'[30]

The relevance of Morris's ideas to the Adams' practice may be further demonstrated by his *Rural Architecture* of 1750, a pioneer volume of schemes for small villas or 'little plain buildings' designed for particular locations such as the South Downs or 'an eminence'. Once again a preference for 'plainness and utility to gaiety and ornament' is maintained. No fewer than three copies of this book found their way into the Adam office, as John, Robert and their father are all listed as subscribers. John Adam's villas in the 1750s clearly reflect the influence of Morris's ideas,[31] as does the mausoleum that he and Robert erected to the memory of their father in Greyfriars churchyard, Edinburgh, in 1753; and it seems probable that Robert Morris also provided the initial inspiration for many of the brothers' smaller classical schemes.

One element deriving from Roger and Robert Morris, the pyramid roof, was to become a leitmotif of Robert and James Adam's own style. Nine of the classical schemes in this volume have such a roof and in one, the pyramid-roofed villa (Pls. 31 and 32), it is the defining feature of the design. A second Morris motif is the square pavilion. In the pyramid-roofed villa and at Kirkdale (Pl. 21) it is given emphasis by four eaves pediments; at Wyreside (Pl. 30) it is treated as a domed cube, while in another design four pediments *and* a dome are fused into one complex roof (Pl. 24).[32] Elsewhere the square pavilion appears as a simple form (Pls. 7, 19, 23, 29 and 34) with shallow slate roofs, overhanging eaves and prominent weathervanes giving an Italianate character which anticipates the work of James Playfair in the 1790s or of John Nash early in the following century.[33]

The façades of the classical villas may be divided into astylar compositions and those that employ an order. Seven of the houses in this volume propose regular tetrastyle porticoes carried through two storeys. Five more make use of a particular Adamesque motif, well shown at Jerviston, Barholm and Congalton (Pls. 6, 23 and 29) where a portico with widely spaced central columns, or perhaps an overscaled aedicule, is fused with a façade to provide the central focus for an elevation. Adam also employs a freely treated giant order at Wyke Manor and in both his schemes for Rosebank. Many of these houses have however other elevations which make no use of columns or entablatures and which depend entirely on proportional adjustments for their effectiveness. The late villas are often shown with a particular type of flat-topped entrance porch, which is supported on slender Tuscan or Roman Doric columns (Pls. 7, 8, 17, 18, 19, 24, 28 and 30), and often where this occurs it is the only indication of an order in a design that is otherwise astylar.

These restrained elevations show certain common approaches. One of them is Adam's tendency to repeat on one floor the pattern of window openings established on another, to provide vertical emphasis. The entrance front of a house like Jerviston (Pl. 6) shows this theme in a simple form. As a motif it goes back to the façade of the Royal Society of Arts building in the Adelphi, designed in 1771,[34] but it remains a standard in the Adam repertoire, orchestrating in a powerful way the cliff-like north façade of the university buildings at Edinburgh, begun in 1789, and providing a coherent visual aesthetic in many of the villas and indeed the castles as well. The pattern, simply stated, appears at the villa based on Lord Delaval's house, at Barholm and Congalton (Pls. 5, 23 and 29) while High Down, Glasserton and Kirkdale (Pls. 11, 17 and 19) develop it in more elaborate ways.

Kirkdale also provides an excellent example of another recurring idea, Adam's quest for duality in the centre of a façade. The architecture of its entrance front exhibits an intentional dichotomy. Here the Doric *porte-cochère* which projects as a central accent on the ground floor is consciously negated by the upper storeys where Adam recesses the central section of the front, denies it any pediment and sets it between more dominant single bay blocks which are emphasized by separate roofs. The same conscious duality appears in the schemes for Sunnyside (Pls. 25 and 28), on the entrance façade of the villa for Captain Pitts (Pl. 7), in the pyramid-roofed design (Pl. 31) and in what is certainly the most extraordinary of all the houses, the triangular villa at Walkinshaw (Pl. 35). This spreading of the focus from the central bays of a front offers another illustration of the extent to which the Adam brothers were developing new forms in their later architecture and in their villa designs. It is hinted at in the unusual garden front of High Down (Pl. 11) with its huge portico *in antis*, lacking the culmination of any pediment, and it is brought to an heroic climax in the entrance front of the university buildings at Edinburgh, where two massive blocks, standing like monumental pylons, flank the triumphal archway that leads to the courtyard beyond.

THE CASTLES

The present volume includes fifteen schemes for a total of twelve clients for houses in what the brothers were to call 'the castle style'. There can be no doubt that these designs rank amongst the most original creations of eighteenth-century European architecture. Though eclectic and synthetic in character, the houses that were built are structures of an extraordinary evocative power. An Adam castle is immediately recognizable as such, with a vocabulary and syntax of its own, rendering precedents irrelevant. The amount of space in the book which the brothers were prepared to devote to their castles is noteworthy, as it reinforces both the significance that they attached to the style and the extent to which commissions for houses in this manner grew in the later years of their practice. Evidently a large number of clients, particularly those in Scotland, were prepared to commission castle-style designs and it is clear from the brothers' promotion of the style

that they considered a castle a new type of building with considerable potential for their practice. [35]

In the later 1780s, when the idea of the book first took shape, very few plans had been published for full-scale houses in a Gothic or neo-medieval taste. No other architect had developed such a consistent and coherent form of alternative architecture, and there can be little doubt that, had the book appeared, the originality of the castle style would have struck contemporaries with force. Just when literary sensibilities were being applied to architecture, as they had earlier been to art, when the towers and battlemented ruins of the English countryside were sought out by antiquarians or devotees of the Picturesque and enjoyed for their associational value, Robert and James Adam planned to offer the public a book of architectural designs with schemes for at least ten castles, of which five had already been built. The timing of the project was perfect.

The style of the Adam castles is unfamiliar. They are not as immediately attractive as the villas and are less easily understood. To critics of the early nineteenth century, obsessed by historical accuracy in a revived architectural style, these Adam designs were simply bad.[36] Arthur Bolton, the brothers' biographer, writes of the castles as a false taste which 'led nowhere' and devotes more space to describing their interiors than to an analysis of their uncompromising façades. What do the castles mean? Were Robert and James Adam, who looked with such clarity at classical antiquity, blind to the real appearance of medieval buildings or was the intention underlying this most personal style different to that which critics have supposed?

None of the castle-style schemes exhibits any features that would normally be associated with Gothic or Gothic Revival architecture. Robert and James had already made designs in the flimsy *Gothick* manner of the mid-eighteenth century[37] and had supervised the building of Roger Morris's great Gothic castle at Inveraray from 1748. The massive rectangular block of Inveraray, with round turrets at each corner and traceried windows in its central tower, may well have acted as a stimulus for their own designs, yet their castle style was to be different. They did not copy the detail of Inveraray nor a contemporary *Gothick* taste, for there are no pointed arches, traceried windows, buttresses or pinnacles in any of their castle designs. Their interiors are classical—in the projects for Barnbougle or Findlater, and at Culzean, elaborately so—and there is not one Gothic feature to be found.[38]

A letter written by Robert to Mrs. Montagu in 1766 about Sir James Lowther's estate provides us with a clue to the possible intention of these castles. Adam had been impressed by the rugged landscapes he had seen in the Lake District, and his enthusiasm is suggested in this letter: 'the style of this part of the country is most remarkable; cloud capped mountains, extensive lawns, rapid rivers and immense forests so happily jumbled together that nothing . . . can convey a just idea of them. . . Sir James seems resolved to impose on me the arduous task of placing a castle upon this his principality. It is a work worthy of the chief artist of Olympian Jove and not for a narrow genius of this world.'[39] What is interesting here is that the associations called into Adam's mind by the idea of a castle in Westmorland are classical Olympian ones, not Gothic. There are no references to medieval architecture, to Ossianic legend—then at the height of its vogue—to border wars or to the ancient national past. Adam's inspiration remains rooted in the classical world. Of the castles which he prepared for Sir James each is developed in terms of a round-arched aesthetic with square and circular towers massed boldly together and laid out on an entirely symmetrical plan.[40] What they suggest is not so much any previous British building as a style that is derived from memories of the vast fortified complex of Diocletian's palace at Split. The palace's many courts, intriguing internal planning and long façades broken regularly by interval towers find more than an echo in the brothers' more extensive castle schemes. The fact that these schemes were unrealizably complex does not deny such origins or rule out the possibility that associations with Roman military architecture may have been present in the architect's mind. Fortifications are not in themselves exclusively medieval, and in an age of neo-classicism it is entirely likely that a man such as Robert Adam should conceive of a castle in Scotland not as a Gothic house but in some sense perhaps as an ancient Caledonian fort.

If some neo-classical ideal inspired the conception of the Adam castle style, its forms may none the less be linked to common eighteenth-century models. As an artist Robert Adam is typical of his century: a new style, or a new direction, is not the result of sudden, unique inspiration or of a single burst of creative activity; it evolves and grows out of the example of others. In the view of eighteenth-century theorists, only experience and a well-stored mind can endow an artist with true originality; or to follow Sir Joshua Reynolds, who was a familiar acquaintance of the brothers, though 'invention is one of the great marks of genius; if we consult experience we shall find it is by being conversant with the inventions of others, that we learn to invent.'[41] This was Adam's practice exactly.

The plans of the Adam castles, though in some cases highly inventive, are clearly linked to normal country house or villa prototypes. The round towers placed in the middle of a garden front develop logically out of a central saloon that is circular or bow-ended (Pls. 40–47, 51, 54, 56 and 58). The plans are symmetrical and many details of the façades are based on earlier architecture. In this respect it is the range of Adam's sources that is impressive, for continental, English and Scottish influences may all be detected within the castle style. From the continent Adam took the massive round towers, fringed with battlements, that appear in Renaissance fortresses, the machicolated wall-heads of fortified cities which, on a reduced scale, provide a characteristic external cornice and, from Renaissance or perhaps contemporary military engineering, the purposeful modelling of a torus moulding adapted to mark a break between a sloping revetment and a vertical wall. One particular Renaissance model, the west front of the ducal palace at Urbino with its tall loggias held between turrets, presents a synthesis of classical detail and a romantic castellar silhouette that anticipates closely the character of the Adam castle style. French châteaux of the sixteenth

century and designs published by the Du Cercean offer similar combinations of classical detail with fortified plans, and it is such a mixed architecture that is exploited at Dalquharran and Culzean (Pls. 52–55) and in several other schemes. In English architecture the brothers held the achievement of Sir John Vanbrugh in high esteem, not for the detail of his great baroque houses, which they considered too heavy, but for their vigorous massing, for the architect's command of outline and for the adjustment of outbuildings and forecourts to contrive an appropriate setting for any design.[42] Vanbrugh Castle at Blackheath which, like an Adam castle, lacks any specifically Gothic motif, is the one building in British architectural history to anticipate the brothers' manner and it is clear that the arrangement of the forecourt and additional buildings at Culzean, Dalquharran, Seton and Airthrey (Pls. 51–57, 60 and 61) is developed on the basis of Vanbrugh's example. Even the sculpturesque modelling of the main block at Seton and the brothers' delight in precisely articulated centralized plans can be seen as part of a Vanbrughian legacy.[43]

To these sources, or perhaps ingredients, of the castle style, two more remain to be added, both of which may take their origins from the brothers' experience in Scotland. In the later castles details of Scottish traditional buildings often appear. Adam makes use of crow-stepped gables, first in the larger two schemes for The Oaks in 1777 (Pls. 40–43), then at Seton (Pl. 56) and at Mauldslie (Pl. 62); at Caldwell he adopts the angle bartizans of Scottish sixteenth-century castles which recur constantly in subsequent castle-style designs; the high-pitched end roofs of the first design for Mr. Stevenson's castle (Pl. 50) derives from a similar source, while at Mauldslie, which was the most Scottish of all the designs, the circular corner turrets appear almost as a quotation from the royal palaces of Falkland and Holyrood. A number of sketch surveys in the Adam office note details from Scottish sixteenth-century buildings which evidently were to play a part in the general conception of the castle style.

From Scotland Robert Adam also drew the inspiration for the romantic element that is such a powerful ingredient in his castles. In later years the architect's favourite pastime lay in the creation of romantic landscape compositions in which barren moors and mountain passes provide a setting for evocative fortresses and hill-top citadels similar in their effects to the architecture that enlivens the middle distance in the paintings of Claude and of seventeenth-century Italian landscape artists.[44] These watercolours by Adam may be part of an accepted European pictorial aesthetic but they are also a personal response to the picturesque quality of the Scottish landscape. To Adam that landscape seemed a proper setting for a castle style. One of his clients, the landscape theorist, Sir John Dalrymple, for whom he was to rebuild Oxenfoord Castle from 1780, made a clear connection between the character of the setting of any building and the style in which it should be built.[45] This idea is close to Robert Morris's notions on the appropriateness of style and setting and, by the end of the eighteenth century, it was a generally respected picturesque principle that fortified or battlemented architecture was the proper complement of mountainous or heroic scenery. As exemplars of the application of such a theory the Adam castles could not be excelled. They are conceived pictorially, and in an age that was dominated by concepts of balance and symmetry are among the earliest buildings to exploit a degree of picturesque irregularity, as in the irregular accents of the pavilions at The Oaks or the supporting buildings at Culzean (Pl. 53).

A final view of how the brothers regarded their castle style is supplied by John Clerk of Eldin, the father of Susan Clerk, who shortly after Robert's death began a critical essay 'A short retrospective view of the state of architecture in Great Britain previous to Mr. Adams time', which was intended to form part of a memorial publication and promised an account of Adam's new style. Clerk shared a number of tastes with his brother-in-law. He was an accomplished amateur etcher both of picturesque views and of Scottish antiquities; he admired Robert's landscape compositions and occasionally travelled with him to visit a distant commission. The opinions he puts forward can thus be taken to represent the architects' own views.

Like so many of the publishing initiatives associated with the Adam family, Clerk's work was left unfinished. His manuscript is brief, little more than an introduction, and it ends without reaching its true topic.[46] References to Culzean, Dalquharran and Mauldslie prove however that the buildings he would have discussed were all castles. Clerk's argument is against the use of Gothic architecture in domestic buildings and particularly on a small scale. At a distance of forty years he and Adam could look with detachment at the style of Inveraray, discussing the absurdity of building a castle in a Gothic style. [47] Gothic was synonymous with religious architecture, but there was another style, the style of a baronial castle 'intended for strength and resistance', which might be copied and could be traced back through the rude art of the Normans— 'where little ornament but great strength and magnitude prevailed'—to works of Roman grandeur and magnificence. It was a feature of these baronial castles that they rarely used, except in their chapels, a pointed arch, for they tended to preserve the earlier circular-headed openings which were ultimately derived from Rome. To Clerk (and to Robert Adam) 'the great and noble remains of castles in every part of this island' were 'stupendous productions' to be viewed with 'admiration as sublimely picturesque and beautiful.' Even in Tudor architecture great houses did not lack the decorations of the old castle: they may have had large windows but 'they were still flanked by towers and surmounted with turrets and battlements.' Baronial architecture such as this could create effects of pomp and grandeur and 'no one ever more completely adopted the spirit of this species of building than Mr. Adam.' If it is not quite clear whether Clerk means that the Adam castles are an invented Scottish equivalent for the Elizabethan style, or that the grandeur of fortified architecture as a whole inspired their style, we are left in no doubt of the enthusiasm with which their architect responded to the idea of fortified architecture. From the age of twenty, when Robert had inherited from his father

the late medieval ruin of Dowhill, his imagination had been stirred by baronial remains. Later when he was abroad, he had recorded medieval buildings pictorially rather than measuring them. It was as Clerk would have it, 'the spirit' of fortified architecture which he had absorbed and which, in the middle of his career, when he was seeking for a fresh domestic style, found powerful expression in his castles.

AN EXPLANATION OF THE PLATES

An eighteenth-century pattern book such as the Adams planned would, after the Introduction, always provide an explanation of the plates before passing to the designs themselves. Technical considerations to do with the production of engraved pages meant that comment and the plans and elevations had to be separate. Nowadays it is easier, and more convenient for the reader, to put the accompanying text opposite the plate to which it applies, yet this does not do away with the need for a further note. A modern reconstruction of a previously unpublished book poses questions which make a prefatory explanation still necessary.

The first design in Volume 46 of the Adam drawings which I consider to have been prepared for publication is the diminutive thatched lodge designed for James Macpherson, who gave it the unlikely Gaelic name of Tullysoul. It is reproduced as Pl. 1 in this publication, exactly as it appears in the Soane Museum, partly because it is a very modest design (and older architectural pattern books usually progress from simple to grander designs) but also as a reminder to myself and the reader that this volume is a reconstruction made up of fragments. In the 1760s James Macpherson claimed something similar for his own publications for it was he who, in *Fragments of Ancient Poetry* and later Ossanic poems, imposed upon his contemporaries some wild translations 'from the Gaelic' which were largely his own inventions; overnight he made a literary reputation, yet, when challenged to produce his sources, failed to counter in any satisfactory way the charge of forgery. In resurrecting the idea of a book that is almost two hundred years old, I would not wish its plates to encounter a similar charge, so the basis on which they have been chosen and arranged will need to be set out.

The reader will by now have accepted or rejected the hypothesis upon which this reconstruction is based. Adam's plans and elevations lie at the core of the argument, yet it must be admitted that most of the 64 plates now published have been assembled *as pages* specially for this volume. As is explained above, at least two scales are common among the drawings intended for publication. While some of the designs reproduced in this volume are taken from the larger-scale drawings, every building represented in a miniature drawing is included, as I believe this scale was the brothers' final choice. Several of the original drawings to either scale are set out on the page with a plan and elevation exactly related as if for publication but most take the form of single drawings on separate sheets. The miniature drawings are usually contained within a standard rectangular frame, (about 5 by 8½ inches) lightly drawn in pencil which may indicate an intended size for the copper plates. Such a size would have made a small book indeed; in arranging the plate pages for this volume, it has been assumed that it was intended to use two or even three plates to a page. None of the miniature drawings originally had a border round it, but many of the drawings to a larger scale were framed by a thin line, which has been adopted here to provide a border for the plates.

The scale of the miniature drawings, though varying slightly, is usually extremely close to the modern measurement of one millimetre to a foot. To enable the drawings to be measured by a reader, each of the miniature designs has been reproduced to exactly this scale or exceptionally, with the largest schemes, to a scale of 0.75 millimetre to a foot. Adam's habit of marking the length of any elevation onto his office drawings has allowed the size of the reproduction of each illustration to be closely controlled. To preserve a visual distinction between the large-scale and the miniature drawings the former have normally been reproduced at a scale of 2 or 1.5 millimetres to a foot.

With a number of designs, particularly amongst the miniature drawings, there are missing plans or elevations for some buildings which could not be properly illustrated from the remaining material alone. Where this has occurred the missing drawings have been made up either by reproducing to a reduced scale plans or elevations taken from other Adam volumes or, where no appropriate drawing exists, by a modern drawing based on the office copies that record the design. In a number of cases where an original plan has been left as a pencil outline or otherwise incomplete, it has been finished as a photographic print and it is this 'completed drawing' that has been reproduced. Though many of the drawings have been 'tidied up' for publication according to the standards set by the cleanest and best-preserved designs, the Adams' architecture has never been altered.

The letters of the alphabet, over-printed on the plans, are modern. As the Adam drawings exist in a 'before letters state' hardly any bear an indication of the use of the various rooms and where they do the information has been merely scribbled in. Normally the names of the rooms would have been added by the letter engraver along with any captions. There are however examples of the use of capital letters and a key both in plans by the Adam brothers and in architectural pattern books of the period. The convention seemed appropriate here.

One final point remains to be made about the plates. The four alternative schemes for a castle for the Earl of Derby are included not because there is any evidence to suggest that they were intended to appear in this late pattern book but because the evidence of the drawings, which are in a different volume and to a much larger scale, is that they were prepared for publication somewhere. I have also included a second scheme for Rosebank, not represented in the miniature drawings, and four more houses—Barholm, Caldwell, Walkinshaw and Wyke Manor—which I have admitted either because they complement the other buildings in the book or for their intrinsic interest. It will be noted (see p. 14) that at least four more designs for houses definitely existed amongst the miniature plans and I trust, in making up this number according to my own taste, I have not acted extravagantly.

The sequence of the plates follows the scheme adopted by the compilers of Volume 46 in placing the classical houses before the castles. Beyond this basic division I have tended to arrange the designs chronologically, starting with the earliest and fitting in those of no known date where their plan or elevational treatment resembles the style of other drawings. As for the plates, these have been made up, with few exceptions, so as to include all the drawings prepared for engraving by the brothers' clerks. Individual pages can, as a result, vary considerably both in arrangement and in the information they provide. Where a full set of plans was to be shown the Adams appear to have favoured a layout that placed the ground floor and first floor on one sheet and the basement and second floor (or attics) on a second sheet: where there are no indications to the contrary it is this pattern that is adopted here. There is however no fixed system. The architectural publications of eighteenth-century Britain for all the elegance of their appearance have a certain haphazard pragmatism which permits one page to have three elevations, a section and no plan and another to contain several plans and a single elevation. In divising the pages of the plates that follow, the practical good sense of bookmen in the age of George III has been of considerable comfort.

COMMENTARIES AND ABBREVIATIONS

The commentaries which accompany each plate are laid out, as far as is possible, according to a standard pattern. Thus the names of buildings and of clients, where known, will be found in the title line. A brief description of the designs follows with a factual statement referring to the number, size and scale of the original drawings from which each plate is composed. Where a design extends to two or more plates it has occasionally been necessary to repeat some of this information on consecutive pages. Generally the fullest factual statement will be found in the first commentary on each design. In these entries the terms *large scale drawing* and *small scale drawing* indicate that the scheme is one for which drawings prepared for engraving exist either to the large or small scale. Inscriptions on these drawings are normally transcribed in full and are preceded by the abbreviation *Insc.* Where other drawings, not directly associated with the Adams' intended book, have been used to complete a plate (or to provide information for a modern drawing) references are given to the volume and sheet numbers where they may be found, though the inscriptions which they may carry are not usually transcribed. For the large scale drawings where a number of pages exist with neat borders which seem to be original, the contemporary museum convention of giving dimensions has been followed. In these height precedes width. Where a plate is a compound of several drawings the dimensions of individual sheets becomes irrelevant. A reader may none the less form an accurate estimate of the size of each original by reference to the scale which is reported twice: in feet and inches as it appears on the original drawings and in millimetres and feet as reproduced in the published plates.

For full details of works cited by author and date in the footnotes and commentaries see the Bibliography. Other books or institutions that recur with sufficient frequency to make an abbreviated reference useful are:

Robert and James Adam, *The Works in Architecture of Robert and James Adam* (London, 1773–79), vols. I, II and (1822) vol. III, referred to as *The Works*;

Sir Charles Elphinston Adam, ed., *View of the Political State of Scotland in the last century; a confidential Report on the Poitical Opinions, family connections or personal circumstances of the 2662 country voters in 1788* (Edinburgh, David Douglas,

1887), referred to as *Report*;

The Complete Peerage of England, Scotland, Ireland, Great Britain and the United Kingdom, new edn., Vicary Gibbs, ed. (London, 1910–59), 20 vols., referred to as *Complete Peerage*;

The Dictionary of National Biography, Stephen Leslie and Sidney Lee, eds. (London, 1908–09), 22 vols., referred to as *D.N.B.*;

Sir Lewis B. Namier and John Brooke, *The House of Commons 1754–1790* (London, H.M.S.O., 1964), 3 vols., referred to as *Namier & Brooke*.

Letters relating to the conduct of Adam's affairs in Scotland (1789–91), National Library of Scotland, MS.19992, are cited here as *Paterson Correspondence*.

The National Monuments Record for Scotland appears as N.M.R.S. and the Royal Institute of British Architects as R.I.B.A.

NOTES

1. For an account of the history of *Vitruvius Scoticus* see the introduction by James Simpson to the facsimile edition by Paul Harris Publishing (Edinburgh, 1980).
2. Robert Adam's years in Italy, including his friendship with Piranesi and various proposals for publications, are fully described in John Fleming's classic study *Robert Adam and his Circle in Edinburgh and Rome*.
3. These plates, each of which is inscribed with the date of publication, were later to be collected into a bound volume of the brothers' works. Their independent earlier existence is none the less beyond question.
4. Op. cit., vol. VI, pls. 45–51—Kedleston, and vol. V, pls. 38–42, 43 and 44, and 9 and 10—Witham Park, Compton Verney and Shelburne House, London.
5. The full title is *The Works in Architecture of Robert and James Adam, Esquires*. Title pages for the first two volumes, issued only when the series was complete, are dated 1778 and 1779. Usually the plates are given two dates, that of the design itself and the date of publication, which was a legal requirement. The Adams who had their designs engraved either by English artists or by Italians in London or Rome, found it convenient to issue the work in folders of eight plates at a time, with five folders, or numbers, to each volume. The complete series runs to 80 plates. Though the dates of the designs vary, some going back to 1761 or 1762, the publication of the individual numbers is usually consistent. In volume I, the first number bears no date of publication; no. 2 was issued in February 1774; no. 3 in June 1774; no. 4 in January 1775; and no. 5 later that year. In volume II nos. 1 and 2 were issued in 1777, nos. 3 and 4 in 1778, while no. 5, the last, is something of a mixed bag with individual dates of publication ranging through 1776, 1778 and 1779. A second edition of the second volume appears to have been issued in 1786. For volume III, see note 8 below.
6. James's theoretical interests are discussed in Fleming, *Adam and his Circle*, pp. 303–11. See also the Preface to the first number of *The Works*, p. 4: 'We intended to have prefixed to our designs a dissertation concerning the rise and progress of architecture in Great Britain. . . . We have made many observations, and collected various materials to enable us to illustrate this curious and entertaining subject; but to digest and arrange these would require more time than we can command amidst the multiplied occupations of an active profession.'
7. James Adam's book on agriculture is the last publication in the lifetime of the brothers. Posthumous illustrations of their work appeared in George Richardson's *New Vitruvius Britannicus* (1802, vol. I)—Glasgow Assembly Rooms and Gosford House, and in C. L.

Steiglitz, *Plans et Dessings Tirés de la Belle Architecture* (1801)—Balavil House.
8. It has sometimes been suggested that evidence for a waning of interest on the part of the Adams may be detected even within the two volumes that they published. This tends to be indicated by the diminishing status of each preface as the books proceed. The first issue of 1773 opens with an impressive parade of opinions and of classical scholarship that continues for a full five pages with a further four pages of comment on the plates. In later numbers of the first volume the prefaces drop to only a page or two with one page for description of the plates. In volume II only the first number has a preface. While it is true that an extended essay is more appropriate to the earlier issues of any series, James Adam as the *author* of this publication could certainly have provided more information in volume II than the perfunctory lists that accompany the plates for the last four numbers. For an account of the third volume of *The Works*, which he considered a 'rechauffé', see Bolton 1922, vol. II, pp. 338 and 354.
9. For Adam's arrangements in Scotland towards the end of his life see Sanderson 1982.
10. The essential facts relating to the history of the Adam drawings are given in Bolton 1922, vol. II, pp. 354–59. For their vicissitudes between the 1790s and 1833 see Tait 1978a.
11. Scottish Record Office, Clerk of Penicuik Papers, G.D. 18/5549/19.
12. Tait 1978a, p. 453.
13. Bolton 1922, vol. II, p. 357.
14. A collection of letters between Paterson and Adam from which these points emerge is in the National Library of Scotland MS.19992. The well-known insistence by William Burn, the late Georgian architect in Edinburgh, that clerks should exercise great care, amounting almost to secrecy, over his drawings, may well have its roots in the attitude of the Adam brothers and in Burn's knowledge of the number of their drawings that 'migrated' into other hands. The architectural style of Burn's father, Robert, has close similarities to the Adam office manner and a Mr. Burn travelled with Robert Adam to visit various sites in 1791.
15. Scottish Record Office, Blair Adam Papers 4/25 [not as cited by Tait 4/197].
16. These notes appear on drawings for Great Saxham Hall, and for Wyreside, Adam Drawings vol. 34, no. 23 and vol. 36, no. 100.
17. This point is made by Bolton 1922, p. 357. Examples are in vol. 36, nos. 5 and 10, labelled 'Whites Chocolate House' though these are houses for the Provost of Kings College, Cambridge, and for the Earl

of Findlater. Among the drawings for Culzean Castle (vol. 37, nos. 1–8), one is described as 'for the Earl of Hyndford' for whom Adam had designed Mauldslie Castle. In vol. 36, nos. 66–71, designs for Rosebank are inscribed 'for [*blank*] Duncan', a case where William Adam did not remember the client's name, John Dunlop.

18. National Library of Scotland, MS, 19992.

19. Not *all* the drawings in volume 46 are of a type prepared for an engraver. The volume is unusual in the neatness of its layout but some of the earlier designs are clearly clients' designs or copies of them. The large-scale designs prepared for engraving are placed irregularly from p. 4; the miniature plans are collected together as a group between p. 53 and 76.

20. The system of listing the contents of the volumes by 'article' and 'pieces' (i.e. the number of drawings) with an index to the page allows this list to be compared closely with the present contents of volume 46. From this it is clear that the two sheets now missing from p. 55 were of a different subject to the Hill House, Putney, or to Glasserton, the other two designs shown on this page. Similarly the four sheets lost from p. 57 are described as two 'unknown' schemes, each of two pieces, while the sheet that is missing below two elevations of Seton Castle on p. 71 proves not to have been a third drawing of Seton, as might be expected, but yet another 'unknown' design on one sheet. Some drawings were evidently lost from this volume before the index was made. On p. 53, where there is now only one miniature elevation of High Down, two other drawings were clearly once attached to the sheet, yet the index only records one, reading '32 Mr. Radcliffe Herts 2 Pieces 54', (Blair Adam Papers 4/25, 'volume 20').

21. Some of the original drawings that were published in *The Works* are preserved in the Soane Museum. Of these the plan and elevation of Mistley church (vol. 41, no. 64), which was engraved by John Roberts (vol. II, no. V, pl. I), is entirely covered with a pinkish black emulsion on the back and is so heavily scored that it is almost cut through along the major lines. Several other drawings are like this. On the other hand the drawing of the section through the Library at Kenwood (vol. 43, no. 5), engraved by J. Zucchi (vol. I, no. II, pl. V), is deeply scored and heavily pricked through but is not dirty on the back. Processes varied from shop to shop. The drawings for Colen Campbell's *Vitruvius Britannicus* in the R.I.B.A. Drawings Collection provide further examples of a variety of types of over-scoring evident in the façade of St. Peter's and the church in Lincoln's Inn Fields (vol. I, pls. 4 and 8).

22. Bolton 1922, vol. II, p. 338, publishes Priestly and Weale's book list of 1823 together with the catalogue of the Adam sales, pp. 324–337.

23. John Crunden, *Convenient and Ornamental Architecture, Consisting of Original Designs . . . from the Farm House to the Most Grand and Magnificent Villa*, 1767. Later editions are 1785, 1788, 1791, 1797 and 1815. In 1769 Thomas Rawlins published *Familiar Architecture; or Original Designs of Houses for Gentlemen and Tradesmen; Parsonages and Summer Retreats* with further editions in 1789 and 1795. In the foreword Rawlins explains that his intention is to supply a book useful for modest families; previous writers 'have formed plans too extensive for the plain villa, the Parochial church, and elegant Mansion' and have 'neglected to render their designs useful and instructive to country builders.' James Adam was a subscriber to this volume.

24. The alternatives for Wyreside and Airthrey Castle were respectively for a castle-style elevation on the same plan at Wyreside and for a completely different classical villa at Airthrey.

25. For the evolution of this most complex design see Rowan 1983.

26. Competition designs for the *Concorso Clementino* and other papal prizes are well reviewed in Helmut Hager, *Architectural Fantasy and Reality: the Concorsi Clementini 1700–1750* (Penn State University, 1982). French designs for 1774 to 1788 are published by Helen Rosenau in 'The Engravings of the *Grands Prix* of the French Academy of Architecture', *Architectural History, Journal of the Society of Architectural Historians of Great Britain*, vol. 3, 1960, pp. 17–179.

27. The fascination which this type of planning had for Adam is further demonstrated by (or may derive from) his acquisition while in Italy of three volumes of designs, evidently intended to be published as a pattern book, by the Milanese architect Giovanni Battista Montano (1539–1621). The first volume contains many geometrical and centrally planned structures. This work, purchased by Sir John Soane at the Adam sale in May 1818, is in the Soane Museum.

28. For the Adams' connection with Roger Morris see Iain G. Lindsay and Mary Cosh, *Inveraray and the Dukes of Argyll* (Edinburgh, 1973).

29. Morris, op. cit., vol. I, p. 119.

30. Morris, op. cit., vol. II, Preface.

31. For John Adam's villas see *Vitruvius Scoticus*, Pls. 45 and 94.

32. This pattern joining pediments and a dome is first used by Adam in a project for Kedleston Rectory and in wings at Combe Bank.

33. For Playfair see *Catalogue of the Drawings of the R.I.B.A.*, Jill Lever, ed., vol. O–R (London, 1974); Colin McWilliam, 'James Playfair's designs for Ardkinglas' in *The Country Seat*, H. M. Colvin and J. Harris, eds. (London, 1970), p. 193, and David Walker, 'Cairness, Aberdeenshire', *Country Life*, 28 January 1971. For Nash's Italianate designs see Terence Davies, *John Nash* (London, 1966) and John Summerson, *The Life and Work of John Nash Architect* (London, 1980) pl. 12A.

34. *The Works*, vol. I, no. IV, pl. IV.

35. Publications on the Adam castle style are: Bolton 1922, vol. I, 'The Castle Style and the First Stirrings of the Gothic Revival', Fleming 1968a and 1968b; 'Robert Adam's Northern Castles', chapter VI in Macaulay 1975; and Rowan 1974a, pp. 679–94, and Rowan 1974b, 1974c and 1974d.

36. 'To unite in the same mass forms so opposite as those which characterise Grecian and Gothic architecture may justly be thought so ridiculous as never to have been attempted' – J. C. London, on Adam's castles, in *Country Residences* (London, 1806), vol. I, p. 115. See also J. M. Leighton on Mauldslie Castle, 'His castellated buildings are all failures' (*Select Views on the River Clyde* (Glasgow, 1830), p. 31).

37. See Fleming 1958b and 'Strawberry Hill and Alnwick Castle', chapter V in Macaulay 1975.

38. Mellerstain in Berwickshire where a corridor and one ceiling are Gothic (1770–78) is the only house which is an exception to this rule.

39. Quoted by Bolton 1922, vol. II, p. 319.

40. Robert and James Adams' schemes for Sir James are published in *Architectural Drawings from Lowther Castle, Westmorland*, H. M. Colvin, J. Mordaunt Crook and Terry Friedman eds., (Society of Architectural Historians, Monograph II, 1980).

41. *Discourse on Art*, no. 6, 1774.

42. Appreciation of Vanbrugh is contained in a footnote (A) on *Movement* added by James Adam to the Preface to the first number of *The Works*.

43. For Vanbrugh's small house plans see H. Colvin and M. Craig, *Architectural Drawings in the Library of Elton Hall by Sir John Vanbrugh and Sir Edward Lovett Pearce* (Roxburghe Club, 1964) and Kerry Downes 'The Kings Weston Book of Drawings', *Journal of the Society of Architectural Historians of Great Britain*, vol. 10 (1967).

44. For Adam's picturesque drawings see Bolton 1925; Oppé 1942; Tait 1971, and Scottish Arts Council 1972.

45. This idea is contained in an important early *Essay* written by Dalrymple for the poet William Shenstone about 1760 and published in 1823 by W. Richardson of Greenwich. For Dalrymple and Oxenfoord see Rowan 1974b.

46. The text is published in full in Fleming 1968b.

47. 'Morris, a minor architect of this country, designed a castle for the Duke of Argyll at Inveraray—not a baron's castle nor even in the Queen Elizabeth style, but a Gothick one—not what he wished it to be but what he was ignorant how to accomplish'. For a detailed study of the building of Inveraray see I. G. Lindsay and M. Cosh, *Inveraray and the Dukes of Argyll*; and Macaulay 1975, Chapter IV.

THE PLATES

Plate 1

Design for a rustic lodge at Tullysoul for James Macpherson, Esquire.

Front and rear elevations, with ground- and first-floor plans, of a low, thatched house linked by short straight wings to detached stable and kitchen(?) blocks. These form a shallow forecourt. The centre of the house is of two storeys with a bowed projection at the back.

Large-scale design. Vol. 46, no. 7. Original dimensions within the margin 368 × 246 mm. *Insc. Tully Soul for James McPherson Esqr*, with sizes of the main rooms, all *12 by 15.*

The frontage extends 52 ft.
Original scale ¾ in. to 10 ft.: here 15 mm. to 10 ft.

This design is unique among those prepared by the Adams for publication as being the only instance of their thatched-cottage manner of which it is a characteristic example. Though rustic in conception the cottage retains a distinctly architectural character. The brothers avoid all meretricious picturesque detail, leaving the deep trim thatch and heavy plain walls—all three feet thick—to speak for themselves. The design is not dated but may be compared with similar thatched schemes for the Duke of Bolton at Hackwood Park (vol. 46, no. 148) of 1777, for the Rev. William Rose at Beckenham (vol. 21, nos. 104–106) and more especially with a lodge designed for the Earl of Wemyss at Gosford in 1790 (N.M.R.S.). Sketches for this scheme are in vol. 10, nos. 75 and 96.

James Macpherson (1736–96) the celebrated translator of the poems of Ossian, like Robert Adam himself, was a Scot who had risen under the patronage of the Earl of Bute, First Minister of George III from 1761 to 1763. Though the authenticity of the great Gaelic epics, *Fingal* (1761) and *Temora* (1763), which he claimed to have discovered was soon challenged, government support for Macpherson, who proved useful as a political writer and polemicist, remained firm. In 1766 he was confirmed in a colonial secretaryship which he held until his death in 1796, and in 1780 he entered parliament as M.P. for Camelford in Cornwall, at about the same time as he was appointed minister or agent in London for Mohammed Ali, the Nabob of Arcot, a post through which he amassed a large fortune. Robert Adam, also an M.P. from 1768, seems to have known Macpherson socially. The architect owned many of his publications and was employed by Macpherson to design castellated additions to a suburban villa at Putney Common, Surrey, in 1785, and a new house at Raitts, Badenoch, Inverness-shire, an estate which he had purchased about 1790. At Raitts Macpherson changed the name of the property to Belleville or Balavil, and it seems likely that Tullysoul, which defies exact location, is a name invented, like so much else, by its proprietor. Bolton lists the property as possibly in Perthshire, the only Scottish county with a quantity of place names with the prefix Tully, which in Gaelic usually signifies a small hill.

(*D.N.B.*; Namier & Brooke, vol. 2, p. 95)

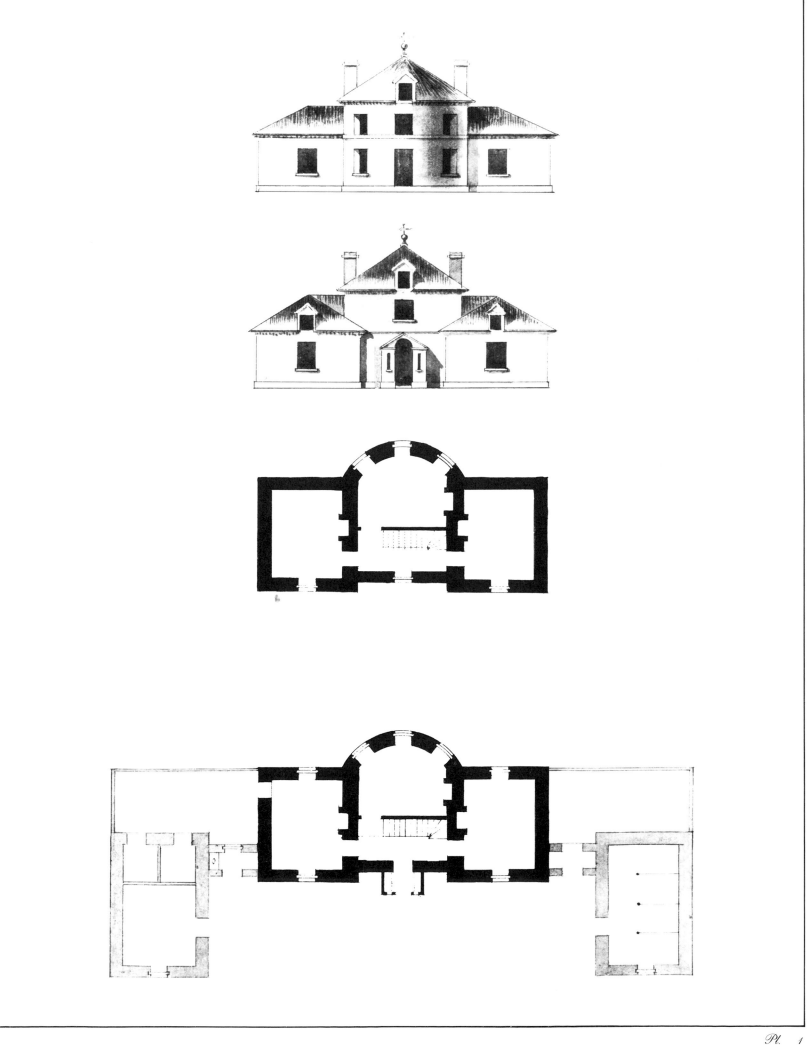

Pl. 1

Plate 2

Design for a miniature villa with 'Pompeiian' two-storey portico.

Front elevation with basement, ground and first floor plans of a rectangular villa with a high hipped roof terminating in a single massive chimney stack.

Large-scale design. Vol. 46, no. 70. Original dimensions within the margin 449 × 274 mm. *Insc. Unknown*. The basement plan given here is completed from a pencil outline on the original drawing.

The frontage extends 42 ft.
Original scale $\frac{7}{8}$ in. to 10 ft.: here 15 mm. to 10 ft.

The interest of this small design resides principally in its portico. Adam here proposes an arrangement of superimposed loggias, reminiscent of the insubstantial architecture of Pompeiian fresco decoration. The unorthodox spacing of the columns and the curious manner in which the upper caryatid order is stepped back, well behind the line of the columns below, both seem to reflect Pompeiian ideas. The scale of this villa is diminutive: three bedrooms and a dressing-room, above two reception rooms, with servants and services tucked out of sight in a 'sunk storey'. Inconsistencies in this design are the ramps leading to the loggia which do not appear in the elevation. Adam also altered the pitch of the roof on this drawing and added a lightly pencilled Tuscan colonnade and terminal pavilion on the right-hand side. The pencilled addition is not reproduced here. The plan adopted here is similar to that proposed in the first version of the villa for Captain Pitts which may be related to this design (Pl. 7). Sketches for this villa proposing side porticoes similar to that of the front are in vol. 1, nos. 132 and 233.

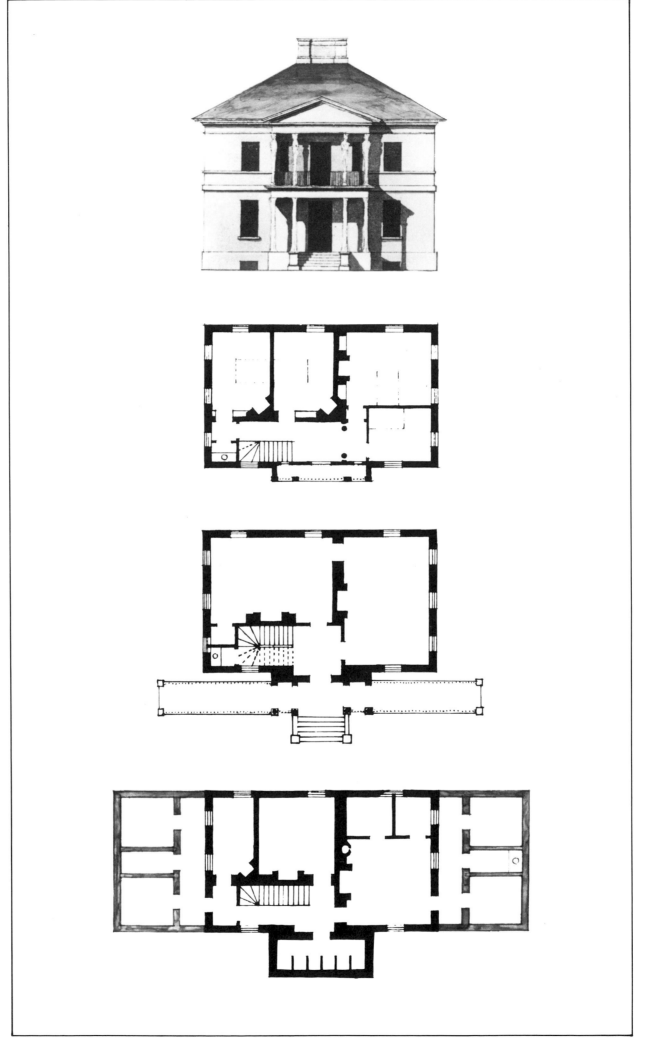

Pl. 2

Plate 3

Design for a villa for James Thomson, Esquire.

Front and rear elevations, with the ground-floor plan, of a small classical house. Rectangular in plan with a wide perron to the entrance front, and a tetrastyle Doric portico above a rusticated basement on the garden façade.

Large-scale drawing. Originally two sheets. Vol. 46, nos. 5 and 6. From these the bedroom-floor plan of no. 5 has been omitted. A border line, added at a later date to match that on the Tullysoul drawing, is 368 × 210 mm. *Insc. James Macpherson Esq, Plan of the . . . story* and, on no. 6, *James Thomson Esq*. The use of the rooms is indicated as follows:

A	Hall	C	Dining-room
B	Drawing-room	D	Study

Three bedrooms with dressing-rooms are accommodated above

The frontage extends 45 ft., and 68 ft. including the perron.
Original scale $\frac{1}{8}$ in. to 1 ft.: here 15 mm. to 10 ft.

The different names written over the two façades of this small classical villa offer a clear instance of the confusion in many of the inscriptions added by the compilers of the volumes of Adam drawings. The two elevations, each with a plan underneath, are patently part of one design, though whether the scheme was prepared for James Macpherson or James Thomson cannot be known. The style of the villa with its plain ashlar walls, minimal detail and low upper-floor windows suggests a date in the 1760s rather than the 1770s or 1780s, which is the period of most of the designs prepared for this publication. As the architects do not appear to have worked for James Macpherson before 1785 (Pl. 1) a preference may be given to James Thomson as the client for whom this design was made. It seems unlikely however that this Mr. Thomson is, as Bolton suggests, the poet and author of *The Seasons* who died in 1748 and for whose monument, in Westminster Abbey, Robert made designs. The spelling of the surname (without the English 'p') and the thickness of the walls on the plan, which suggests a stone house, seem to indicate a Scottish origin for the design.

In scale and layout this villa is not unlike some earlier Adam family work: Fala House by William Adam or John Adam's town villas for Lord Milton or Lord Alemoor (*Vitruvius Scoticus*, pls. 121, 45 and 123). It is a modest design, yet the absolute purity of the rectangular block from which it is composed, the broad ramp that leads to its main door (shielding the basement offices on the entrance front) and the Doric portico that is the only feature on the rear elevation, each exhibits a concern for unambiguous and clearly expressed form that gives the building its distinctive quality. While the interior limitations of such a simple box are clear, variety is supplied by the apse in the hall that faces the front door and by the wide segmental recess at one end of the dining-room which skilfully adjusts the balance of a room that would otherwise have been irregular. This is exactly the sort of refinement at which the brothers excelled, turning to their advantage a defect in order to increase the interest of the interior space and provide, in the very room that needs it, a convenient china closet.

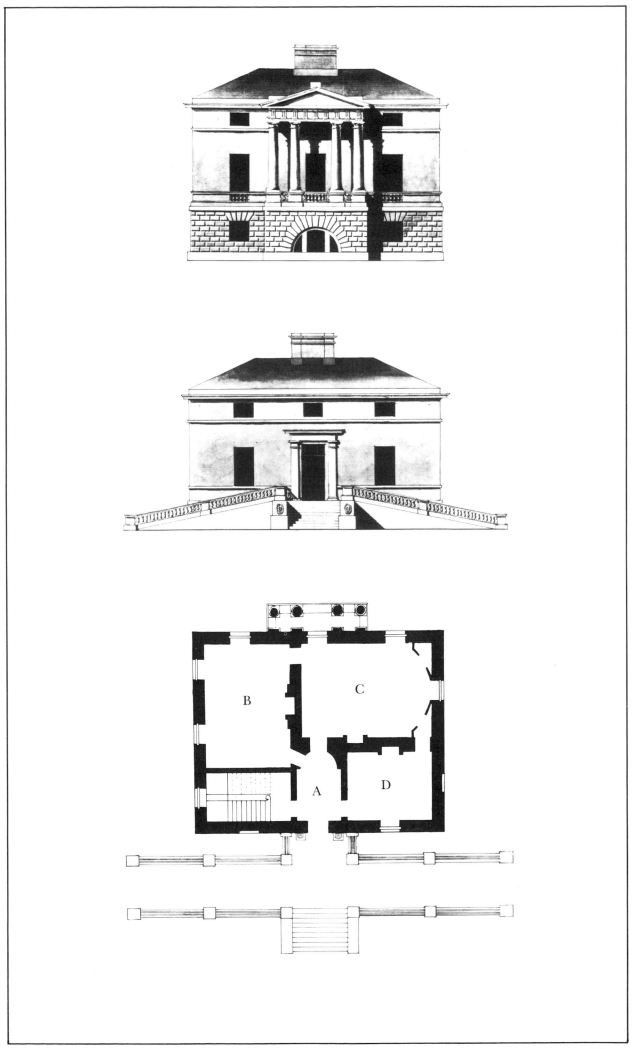

Pl. 3

Plate 4

Design for a classical villa.

Front and rear elevations with the ground-floor plan of a small three-storey house, with a tetrastyle Ionic portico on the garden front.

Large-scale drawing. Originally two sheets. Vol. 46, nos. 42 and 43. From these the plan of the basement, only partially completed on no. 43, has been omitted. The original border line on both sheets is 421 × 255 mm. *Insc. Unknown* with some pencil indications of the use of the basement rooms.

The frontage extends 60 ft.
Original scale 1 in. to 10 ft.: here 15 mm to 10 ft.

In comparison to the villa shown on Pl. 3, the style of this design, though severe and lacking in decoration, is clearly in a later idiom. The arrangement of the rooms in an irregular cruciform plan is characteristic of the architects' interest in the articulation and massing of an architectural design. The accommodation provided in this villa may be modest yet the structure would have had a certain geometric authority. The arrangement of the villa as a house that is to be built into a sloping site—two storeys over a semi-basement on the entrance front and three storeys on the garden front—is also worthy of note. This formula is often adopted in Adam villa designs and was to become a standard of country-house practice in Scotland in the early nineteenth century. The internal planning, a straightforward arrangement of smallish rectangular rooms, may be compared with the villa designed for Captain Pitts of 1783 (Pl. 7) and with the anonymous design of a house with a pyramid roof (Pl. 31).

    On the garden front the tetrastyle giant-order portico of closely grouped Ionic columns is comparable to the Adam wing at Nostell Priory of 1776 and similar to Adam's alterations to David Garrick's villa at Hampton of 1775. The first scheme for Dr. Turton's villa at Brasted of 1784 also envisaged an Ionic portico of this character (see notes to Pls. 8, 9 and 10) and gable pediments on the side elevations as here. The thickness of the walls in the plans suggests that the villa was to have been built in brick.

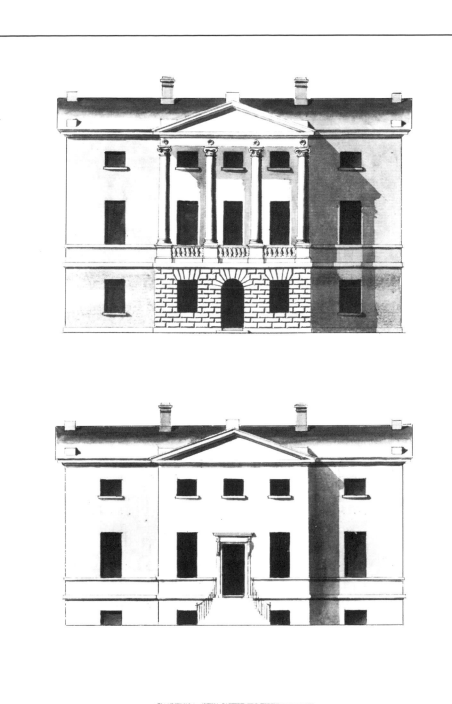
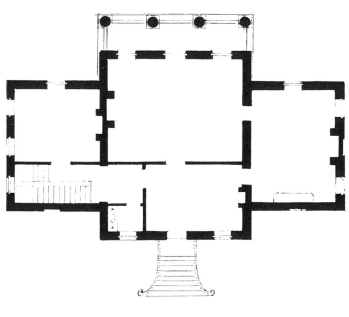

Pl. 4

Plate 5

Design for a small country villa and an elevation of the principal front of a house designed for Princess Isabella Lubomirski.

Entrance front and rear elevation with the plans of the basement, principal floor and bedroom floor of a miniature villa. A cruciform plan developed round a square central stairwell, with a bow in the middle of the garden front and a projecting, pedimented entrance block. Also a larger version of the front with pavilions and arcaded wings.

Small-scale drawings. Vol. 46, nos. 100 and 101. The plate is composed from these two sheets. *Insc. Unknown*, and a third drawing to a larger scale *Insc. Principal front of a Villa for the Princess Lubomirski*, vol. 36, no. 90.

The frontage of the small design extends 46 ft.; the larger is 158 ft.
Original scales 1 in. to 21 ft. and $\frac{7}{8}$ in. to 10 ft.: here 13 mm. to 10 ft. and 10 mm. to 10 ft.

The villa recorded here is a reduced version of Milburn, Claremont Lane, Surrey, a design commissioned about 1786 by the first Lord Delaval. The schemes for Lord Delaval's villa come first in vol. 46, (nos. 1–4). They are to a large scale and have the appearance of perhaps being intended for publication, though the shape of the drawing sheets and the rather unsystematic arrangement of plans and elevations leaves this in doubt. The first design proposed flanking single-storey square pavilions linked to the main block by a straight sunk corridor. Subsequently Adam proposed larger cross-shaped wings fused directly with the main block (vol. 34, nos. 104–07).

Sir John Hussey Delaval (1728–1808), whose principal seats were Ford Castle and Vanbrugh's Seaton Delaval in Northumberland, was M.P. for Berwick when Adam represented Kinross. In politics he was a close associate of the Duke of Northumberland, probably the Adam brothers' most magnificent patron. He was created Baron Delaval in the Irish peerage in 1793 by Fox and caused something of a sensation by voting for Pitt in 1786 when he was rewarded by the United Kingdom title of Baron Delaval of Seaton Delaval. His employment of Adam seems to date from this time, and the house, though now much altered, was built between 1787 and 1790 (Namier & Brooke, vol. 1, p. 311; *The Complete Peerage*, vol. 4, p. 138).

Soon after it had been designed, 'Lord Delaval's house in the country' reappeared in the Adam office as a villa of the Princess Lubomirski, a Viennese celebrity, wife of the Grand Marshal of the Crown in Poland, who was in England in 1787. For the princess, the sunk corridors of Lord Delaval's design were elevated to become arcaded three-bay wings connecting the pavilions to the main block, with a bath and changing rooms on one side and a conservatory and library on the other. This enlargement, shown here in the principal elevation, represents the greatest degree of elaboration given by Adam to the basic design. Isabella Lubomirski perhaps intended the house as a trianon for her husband's estate of Lańcut near Rzeszow in southern Poland, where from 1780 she had been redecorating the castle to designs of the Italian Vincenzo Brenna with the help of two Polish architects, S. B. Luz and J. C. Kamsetzev. Nothing is known of Adam's villa at Lańcut. (M. H. de Marsue, Marquis of Ruvigny, ed., *The Titled Nobility of Europe* (London, 1914), p. 951).

A sketch of a domed villa deriving from the basic elevation of the main block (vol. 1, no. 228) with further variants of the design (vol. 1, nos. 114–16) and the set of drawings prepared for publication attest Adam's continuing fascination with the potential of this neat miniature scheme. In the villa drawn up for inclusion in the book one new element, not envisaged in the earlier prototypes, is the detached kitchen block sunk into the ground and linked to the basement by a dog-leg passage running under the lawn on the garden front. Adam made similar proposals in designs for Robert Trotter, for additions to The Bush outside Edinburgh in 1791 (vol. 35, nos. 84–92); this last version of Lord Delaval's and Princess Lubomirski's villas probably dates from the same period.

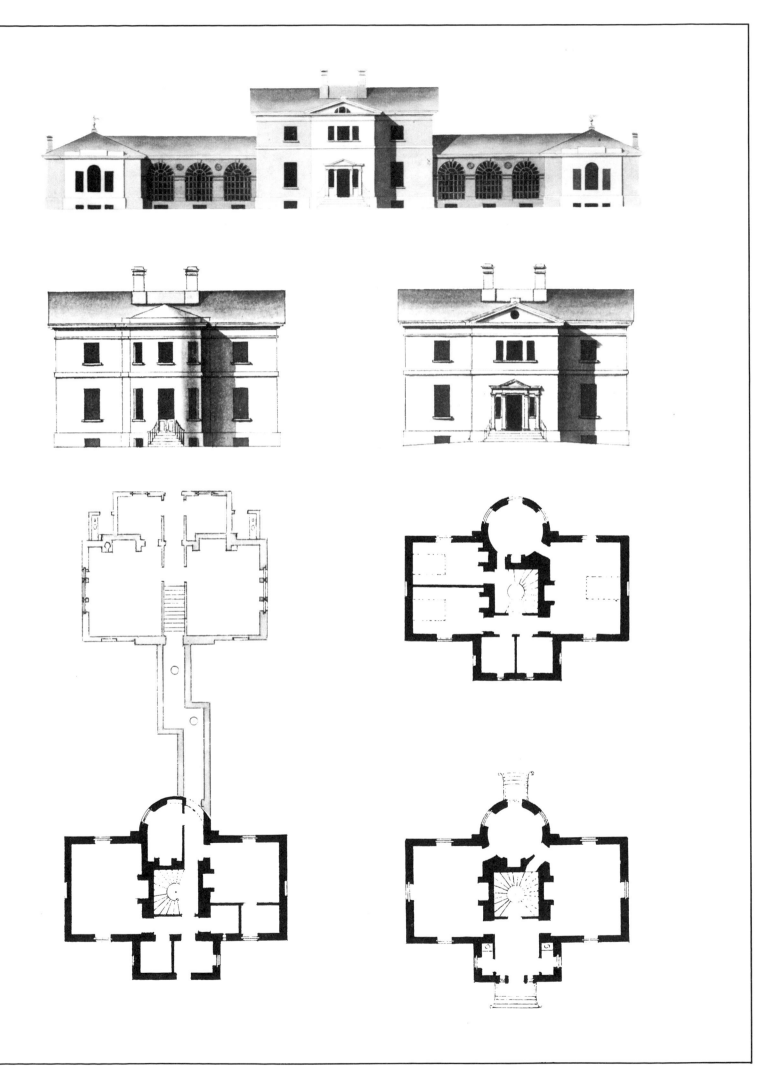

Pl. 5

Plate 6

Design for Jerviston House, Holytoun, Lanarkshire, for James Cannison, Esquire.

Front and rear elevations, with plans of the ground- and first-floor levels, of a small country house with a centre block, straight corridor links and low rectangular wings. In the centre of the entrance front paired Tuscan pilasters flank a relieving arch with a shallow pediment above; this motif is repeated to a smaller scale in the centre of each wing.

Small-scale drawings. Originally two sheets, each of one plan and one elevation. Vol. 46, Nos. 93 and 94. *Insc. Mr. Cannison.* The use of rooms indicated on the design plans in vol. 42, nos. 42–47, is as follows:

A	Hall	F	Dining-room
B	Gentleman's Dressing-room	G	Drawing-room
C	Kitchen	H	Breakfast room
D	Butler	I	Kitchen court
E	Servants' bedroom	J	Dairy court

The frontage extends 177 ft.
Original scale 1 in. to 25 ft: here 10 mm. to 10 ft.

Design drawings for Jerviston are dated 12 Feb. 1782. The house, demolished in 1966, was built almost exactly as it is shown here, the only alterations being to the wings where a Diocletian window, with a tripartite opening immediately below, took the place of the plain window under the pediment. Shallow hipped roofs were also added instead of the flat roofs of these drawings and the rear elevation was left as a plain wall. The front of the house was built of polished ashlar sandstone and the sides and garden elevation of squared coursed rubble with raised nibs or frames at the corners and round the windows, suggesting that it was intended to harl the building. This was never done. Weathering and staining on the wings were much more marked than on the main block of the house which probably means they were built of a different sandstone brought from a different bed and at a later date. If this is so, the alterations made to the design of the wings were probably not the work of Adam.

(Illustrated in R. Strong, M. Binney and J. Harris, *The Destruction of the Country House* (1974), p. 217)

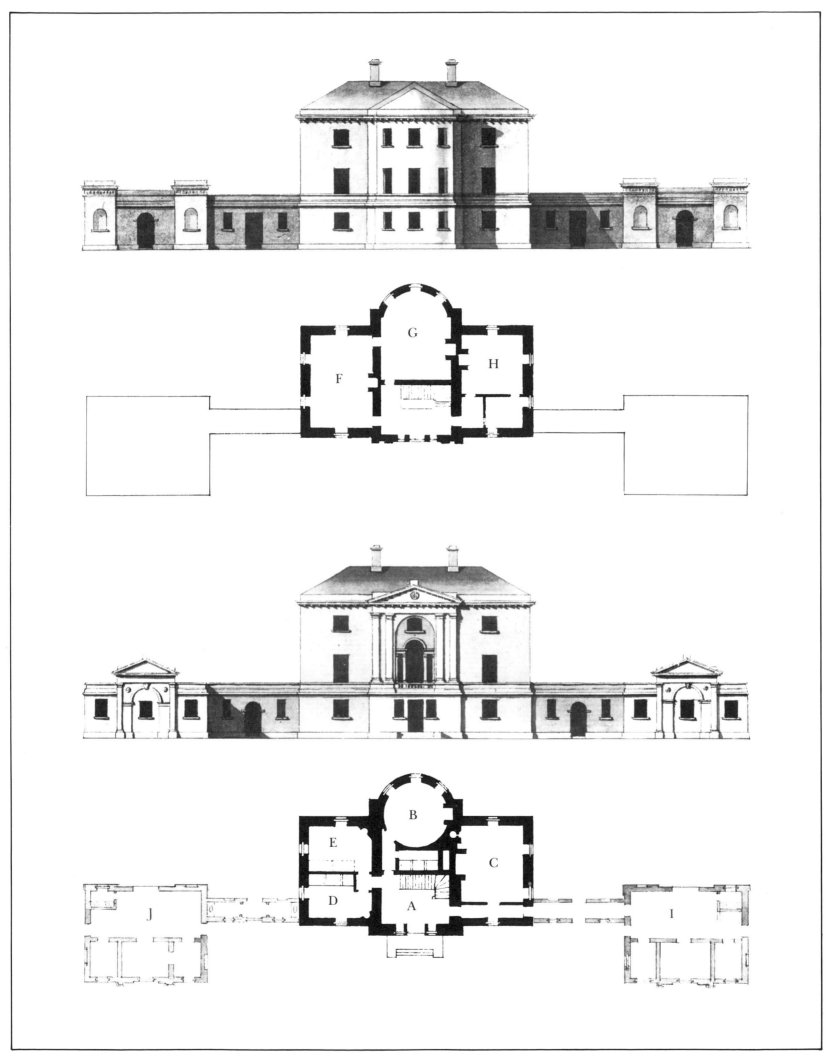

Pl. 6

Plate 7

Design for a villa for Captain Pitts.

Front and rear elevations, with plans of the principal and bedroom floors, of a small villa with wings: a rectangular main block, long and straight Tuscan colonnades and cube-like end pavilions with shallow pyramid roofs.

Small-scale drawing. Originally two sheets, each of one plan and one elevation. Vol. 46, nos. 91 and 92. *Insc. Unknown.* The use of the rooms, indicated on the design drawings in vol. 45, nos. 78 and 79, is as follows:

A	Hall	E	Study or Book-room
B	Eating-room	F	Bedrooms
C	Captain Pitts' Dressing-Room	G	Gardener's room
D	Brewhouse		

The frontage extends 193 ft.
Original scale 1 in. to 25 ft.: here 10 mm. to 10 ft.

Designs for Captain Pitts' villa are dated 2 May and 22 May 1783. Those of the earlier date show a house that is essentially similar to this reduced copy design but a little more elaborate: on the entrance front the colonnades linking the small pavilions to the house are arcaded with coupled pilasters to each pier and the position of the round-headed and flat-headed windows on the pylon elements flanking the entrance porch is reversed; the garden façade has rather obtrusive Venetian windows fitted within the advanced flat bays of the ground floor instead of the simple form used in this design. The plan too was slightly different, with Captain Pitts' dressing-room and the staircase changing places and the projection beside the eating-room forming a part of the room in the first design.

The bedroom floor plan, dated later in the same month, is identical to that published here and it may be assumed that this design was fixed in its present form by 22 May 1783. The conscious duality of the main façade with paired single-bay pylons flanking the large central window is a characteristic, and much copied, late Adam device: by contrast the square pavilions with their shallow pyramid roofs, though often repeated, go back to the Adam family mausoleum in Greyfriars Churchyard, Edinburgh, designed by John Adam in 1753.

The accommodation proposed for Captain Pitts's villa suggests a bachelor establishment. A captain in the Royal Navy might seem a likely person to employ an expensive architect like Robert Adam, but there is no record of any Captain Pitts in the navy lists for this period. Adam's client may possibly be identified as Matthew Pitts, appointed a captain in the Corps of Engineers on 7 May 1779 (*A List of the Officers of the Army to June 1786* (Dublin, James King, 1786), p. 156) and entered as a captain-lieutenant in the Plymouth Division in the warrant list of 1784 (Whitworth Porter, *History of the Corps of Royal Engineers* (London, 1889), vol. 1, pp. 213–15). If the villa were designed for him, he may have intended it as a place of retirement, as in 1788 he applied for and obtained a vacant captaincy in the Invalid Corps of the Royal Engineers which he held until 1797. The Invalid Corps, established in 1784, was a body of seven semi-retired officers and was intended for men who, through age or infirmity, were no longer fit for action in their profession. They entered the Corps with the rank and pay they held at the time of retirement, a privilege which Captain Pitts was to enjoy for nine years. This villa does not appear to have been built.

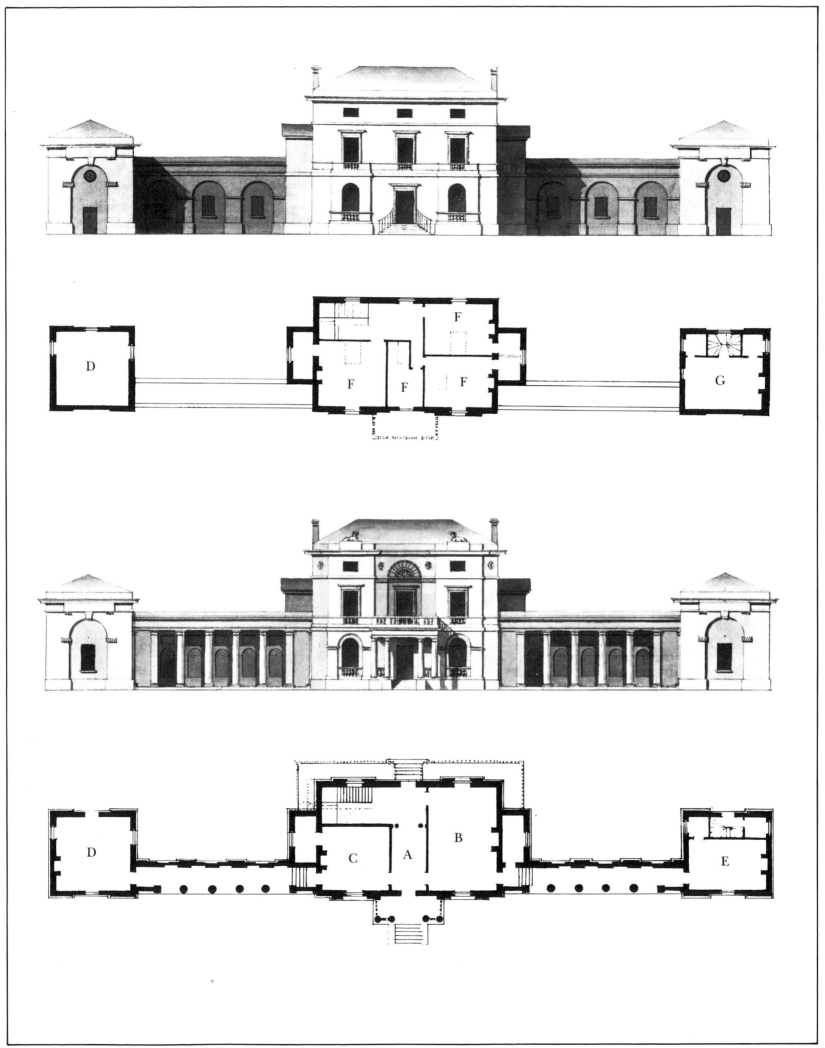

Pl. 7

Plate 8

Design for Brasted Place, Brasted, Kent, for Dr. John Turton.

Front elevation and the plans of the principal floor, first floor and attic of a rectangular villa with a Tuscan porch on the entrance front and an asymmetrical wing to the right.

The designs for Brasted Place, preserved in vol. 46, nos. 130 and 131, are drawn to an intermediate scale almost twice the size of the small designs but not as big as the large-scale drawings. Light pencil borders round both these elevations measure 125 × 212 mm. and correspond exactly with the borders of several of the small-scale drawings prepared for publication. It would seem therefore that in some cases the brothers intended to use a larger scale for particular schemes and that Brasted Place was to appear in the book in bigger images. This intention has been respected in the plates that follow. In vol. 46 one sheet has been torn away and is here replaced by the design drawing of the main floor plan and the two upper floors, vol. 42, nos. 73, 74 and 75. No. 130 is inscribed *Unknown front*. The use of the rooms is as follows:

A	Hall	E	Bedchambers	I	Maid's room
B	Study	F	Dressing-rooms	J	Men's room
C	Eating-room	G	Continuation of the kitchen	K	Cook's room
D	Drawing-room	H	Servant's rooms		

The frontage extends 55 ft.
Original scale $\frac{3}{4}$ in. to 10 ft.: here, elevation 15 mm. to 10 ft.; plans 10 mm. to 10 ft.

The earliest drawings for Brasted Place, for which Adam was to prepare three separate sets of designs, date from 5 August 1784 (vol. 42, nos. 87–90 and vol. 10, nos. 84, 194–197). These record a long, seven-bay, three-storey house set against a steeply sloping site so that the garden front is of only two storeys. This design, like many of Adam's first thoughts, has a certain looseness to it and was larger than Dr. Turton required. It was replaced by a second project (see Pl. 10), designed for an alternative site further north and on flat ground where the same level could be maintained on both fronts. Dr. Turton, who was childless, evidently thought this second scheme was still too large, and the house was further reduced to the modest frontages shown here. The design drawings relating to this final reduced scheme are in vol. 42, nos. 68–75. None is dated. A pencil outline of the north front showing anthemion and palmette decoration continued across the entire length of the frieze is in vol. 1, no. 109. The full plans of the house as built are published in Bolton 1922, chapter 27.

The relationship between Robert Adam and his doctor, John Turton (1735–1806) was a close one. Turton like Adam was at the top of his profession, physician to the king and reputedly a particular favourite with Queen Charlotte. When he moved into the brothers' Adelphi development in the 1770s, his patients included a number of well-known Adam clients: the actor David Garrick, the Earl and Countess of Mansfield, and one of Robert Adam's staunchest supporters, Lord Frederick Campbell, the younger brother of the Duke of Argyll. It was from Lord Frederick, for whom Adam had already made additions at Combe Bank in Kent, that Turton purchased in 1784 the adjoining estate of Brasted, where his country villa was to be built (*D.N.B.*).

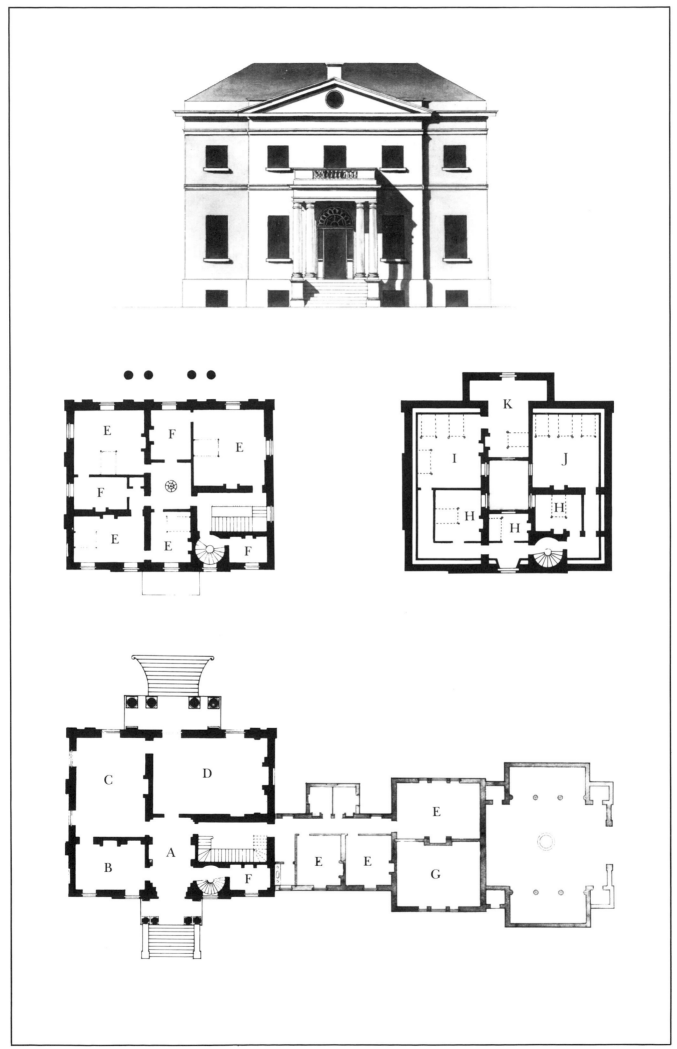

Pl. 8

Plate 9

Design for Brasted Place, Brasted, Kent, for Dr. John Turton.

Side and rear elevations showing a tetrastyle Ionic portico on the garden front with Ionic corner pilasters.

Medium-scale drawing. Vol. 46, no. 131. The side elevation. *Insc. Unknown side view.* The rear façade is taken from vol. 42, no. 68.

The frontage extends 55 ft.
Original scales $\frac{3}{4}$ in. to 10 ft. and 1 in. to 10 ft.: here 15 mm. to 10 ft.

The side and rear elevations shown here bear evident traces of the cutting down that Adam was forced to accept in completing this commission. The scale of the portico is too large for the modest extent of the façade in its final form while the single pilaster at the left-hand end of the side elevation reads curiously where the central arched motif has been reduced to a projection of only a few inches. It is also worth noting that the irregular side wing of bedrooms and domestic offices added to the west of the house is not shown in the elevations prepared for publication. It appears in two outline elevations in vol. 10, nos. 196 and 197. In this design Adam evidently intended to mark the difference between the villa and its appurtenances by a contrast between an architectural enrichment that is highly finished and absolute plainness.

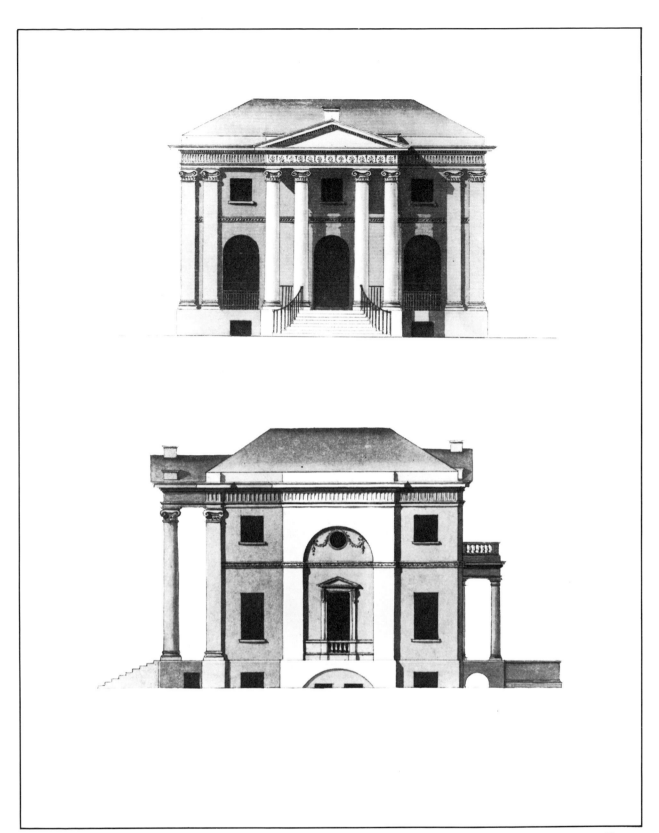

Pl. 9

Plate 10

Another design for Brasted Place, Brasted, Kent, for Dr. John Turton.

Front and rear elevations of a large rectangular villa; the outer bays checked back from the front and treated as square projections on the sides.

Large-scale drawing. One poorly finished elevation of the entrance front of this scheme is in vol. 46, no. 66. *Insc. Unknown.* The drawings illustrated here are taken from vol. 42, nos. 76 and 77.

The frontage extends 95 ft.
Original scale 1 in. to 10 ft.: here 15 mm. to 10 ft.

There can be little doubt that the elevations shown here record Adam's preferred scheme for Brasted Place. The rectangular mass of the projecting end bays give this design a weight and authority which, if not quite lacking, are greatly reduced in the cut-down scheme that was built (Pls. 8 and 9). These imposing façades, at a length of 95 ft. have more than sufficient breadth, to balance the tall Ionic portico of the garden front and to support the broad pediment on the north which, in the reduced design, looks pinched and almost mundane. It was cost that brought this scheme to nothing: 'the design done previous to the one fixed upon to be carried into execution', Dr. Turton wrote to Adam, 'might show your genius where you were not shackled by expense; but it could never have been supposed, even under your own ideas, to be such a plan as I was likely to adopt when the expense of executing it would have been eleven thousand pounds' (Guildhall Library, London, MS. 3070).

Though details of the decoration in these designs are patently neo-classical, the form of the portico itself, with closely set outer columns and a wide central space, offers a clear indication of the range of the architect's borrowings: the source of this unorthodox intercolumnation—which Adam was often to adopt in these designs (Pls. 3, 6, 27, 33 and 34)—is not found in antiquity but in baroque Rome, and more particularly in the twin churches of S. Maria dei Miracoli and S. Maria in Monte Santo by Bernini, whose theatrical arrangement in the Piazza del Popolo appealed to the town planner in Adam, who had sketched their layout while he was abroad. Brasted was not to be built in this form, yet elements of the grand scheme recur in later works. The succession of triple Venetian windows across the garden front was to reappear at Gosford House in East Lothian in 1790, while the composite central focus of the entrance front with its four-columned Doric porch and Diocletian window above finds more than an echo in the symmetrical blocks of houses that flank St. George's church in Charlotte Square, Edinburgh.

Pl. 10

Plate 11

Design for a new house at High Down, Hitchin, Hertfordshire, for Mr. John Radcliffe.

Plan of the principal floor, with elevations of the entrance and garden fronts, of a large country house with pedimented wings.

Small-scale drawing of the entrance façade. Vol. 46, no. 90. *Insc. Mr. Radcliffe Herts*. This drawing is on a left-hand page in the volume with space below for two similar sheets, traces of the corners of which remain. These would be nos. 90a and 90b and from their measurements it would appear that 90a—essentially the same shape and size as 90—was a drawing of the garden front while 90b, which was deeper, was a plan of the house. The garden front given here is a modern drawing copied from the outline design in vol. 29, no. 42. The plan is a completed version of the outline drawing in vol. 29, no. 47. The use of the rooms is as follows:

A	Hall	E	Drawing-room	I	Lady's dressing-room
B	Saloon	F	Library	J	Gentleman's dressing-room
C	Dining-room	G	Upper part of kitchen	K	Maid servants bedroom
D	Breakfast room	H	Principal bedroom		

The frontages extends 218 ft.
Original scale 1 in. to 25 ft.: here 7.5 mm. to 10 ft.

This design for a large mansion house of a Palladian character probably dates from 1772, in which year John Radcliffe paid the brothers £140 in September and a Mr. Nasmith, their foreman, a further £26. 16s. 0d. in December. The house was not to be built though the brothers apparently designed the classical additions that Radcliffe made to Hitchin Priory about 1773. Alternative proposals for a castle-style house at Hitchin were also prepared. None of the drawings for these various schemes is dated: A. T. Bolton (Bolton 1922, vol. 1, pp. 37 and 43) attributes the designs to much too early a date in the Adams' career and published this house as dating from the early 1760s. While the garden front, with its regular tetrastyle portico, is typical of the refined Palladianism of Adam's early period—compare for example Bute House in London—the emphatically horizontal entrance loggia of the main front, contained between pylon-like projections, indicates a new taste and style of composition that marks many Adam schemes in the later 1770s and 1780s. Other elements that were to remain favourite motifs in the later works are the Diocletian windows on the ground floor set under Venetian windows and the two-storey apsed motifs in the links to the wings on the garden front. The geometry of the plan with almost identical apsed rooms arranged axially about a pair of oval, top-lit staircases reflects Adam's interest in ideal planning and also perhaps the legacy of Vanbrugh's design methods.

   The scheme for battlemented additions to Hitchin Priory (vol. 29, nos. 49–53) is possibly more in keeping with Bolton's proposed date for these designs, though it might also be compared with Adam's castle-style work at Whitehaven Castle of 1768 and at Mellerstain of 1770. The west front of this castle-style design is published in Rowan 1974d, p. 680.

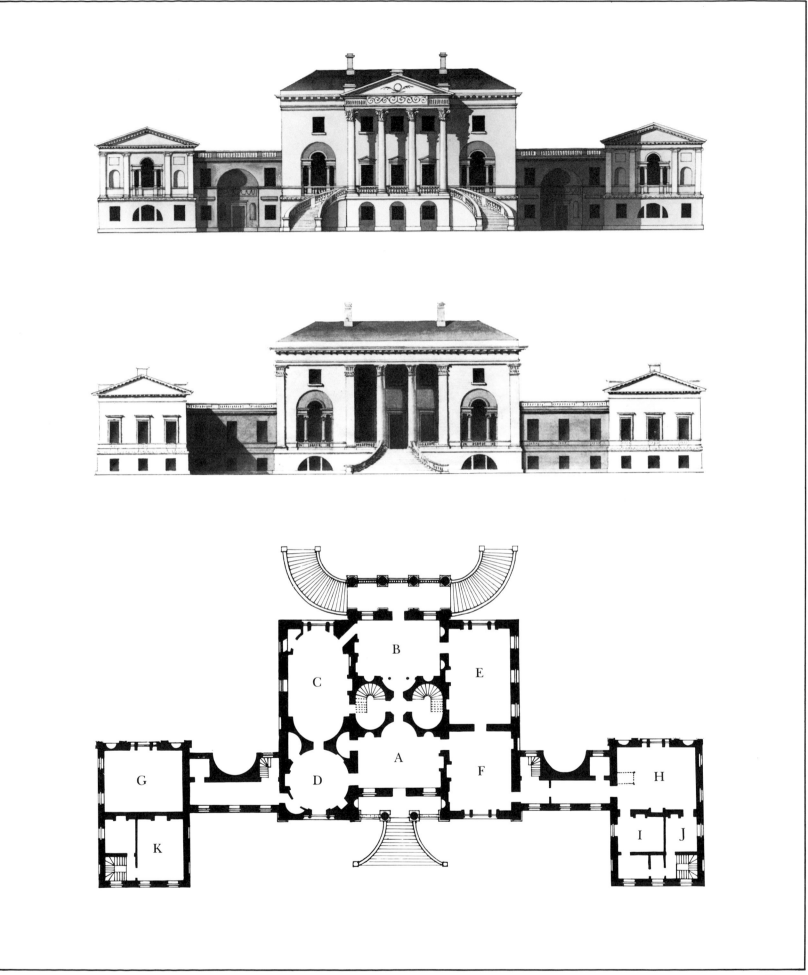

Pl. 11

Plate 12

Designs for a new house at Cadland, Fawley, Hampshire, for the Hon. Robert Drummond.

Plan of the principal storey and entrance front of a large Palladian house with a giant-order, tetrastyle Ionic portico, straight wings and pedimented end pavilions. A circular saloon is in the centre of the garden front. Also the plan and entrance elevation of an alternative smaller design.

Small-scale drawings. Originally on two sheets. Vol. 46, nos. 120 and 121. *Insc. Unknown.* The alternative scheme is shown by modern drawings based on the design drawings in vol. 45, nos. 70, and 73. The use of the rooms in both designs is as follows:

A	Hall	E	Library	I	Dressing-rooms
B	Dining-room	F	Book-room	J	Powder-rooms
C	Drawing-room	G	Butler	K	Kitchen
D	Breakfast room	H	Principal bedchamber		

The frontages extend 192 ft. and 50 ft.
Original scale 1 in. to 25 ft.: here 10 mm. to 10 ft.

The Adam designs for Cadland in the Soane Museum (vol. 45, nos. 70–77) are only partly identified by the inscriptions 'House for (blank) Drummond Esq.' and '2nd design of a house for (blank) Drummond Esq.' The first design, which is the smaller, is dated 10 September 1773 and is evidently intended for a site on the crest of a hill as there is a considerable drop between the front and the back of the house. The Adams kept their account as architects with Drummond's Bank and in 1777 Robert carried out alterations to their premises at Charing Cross. These designs are almost certainly for the Robert Drummond who owned Cadland. The lavish provision for a private wing suggests the wealth of a banking family, while the sloping site matches exactly that of Cadland overlooking Southampton Water. Neither of the Adam schemes was built, as Robert Drummond chose a design by Brown and Holland on which work was begun by July 1775 (Dorothy Stroud, *Henry Holland* (1966), p. 39). The Holland house was demolished in 1953.

Adam's first scheme for Cadland, very much on the scale of a marine villa, is curiously simple: a cubic block of stone set at the edge of falling ground with a very plain front. Indeed the main door of this design, a standard motif in Adam speculative developments in London, gives the house a distinctly urban air, which is only partly offset by the pyramid roof and massed chimneys. The elaboration of the interior with its variety of room shapes is perhaps a surprise, though the planning clearly reflects Adam's experience and success in the design of town houses at this time.

The larger design for a fully developed late Palladian composition promised a house of elegance and considerable richness. Sketches for the main floor plan and possibly for the rear elevation (vol. 10, nos. 168, 169 and 180) show Adam experimenting with ideas taken from his contemporaries: an apse flanked by circular stairs in the main hall as used by Sanderson at Kirtlington Park, and segmental recesses in the corridors of the wings which John Wood had employed at Buckland (see *Vitruvius Britannicus*, vol. IV, pls. 33 and 91). None the less, the principal novelties of the house—a circular dining-room, breaking forward on the garden front and a variety of apsed, oval and circular rooms—are typical of Adam's planning at this date. Two noteworthy features in this design are: the complete separation of the family wing from the main block of the house, an aspect of country-house planning which developed more fully in the early nineteenth century; and the odd arrangement of the portico whose columns are pushed back almost to the line of the façade yet stand in front of it, creating the effect of a portico *in antis* while not quite being one. Such an arrangement is very rare in eighteenth-century architecture, though John Adam had employed a portico of this type at Paxton House, Berwickshire, in 1758 (see Rowan 1967b, 17 and 24 August).

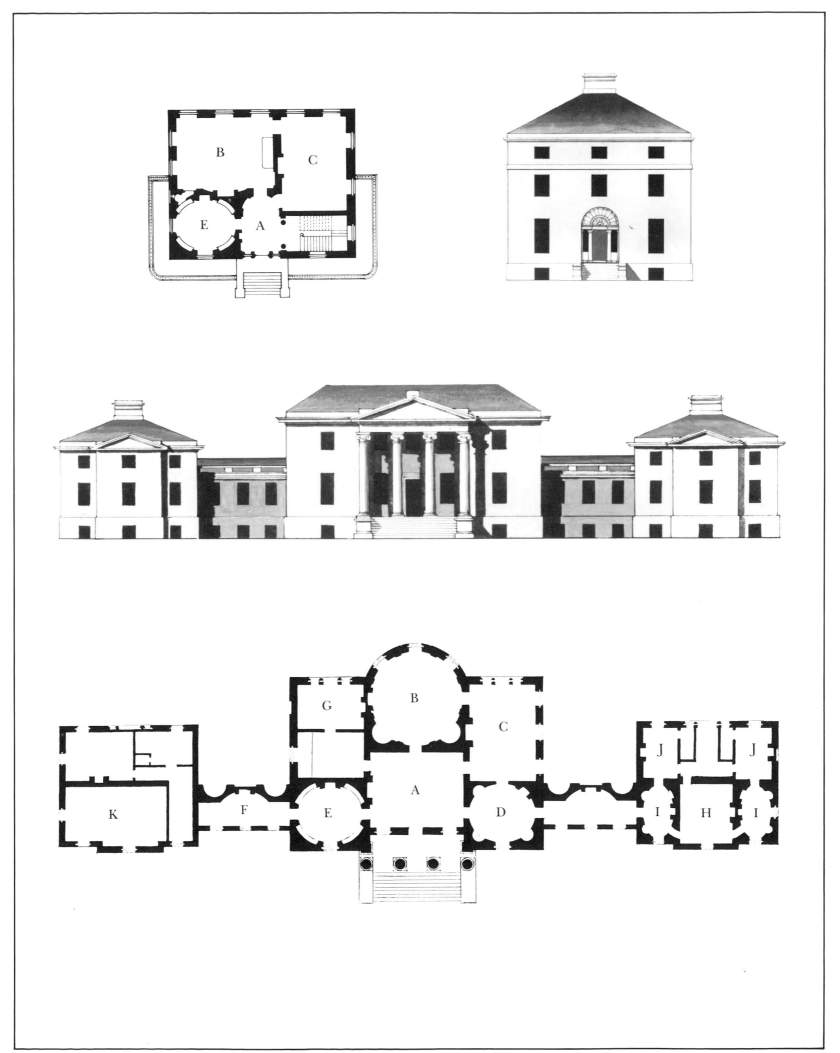

Pl. 12

Plate 13

Design for a new house at Great Saxham, near Bury St. Edmunds, Suffolk, for Hutchinson Mure, Esquire.

Plan of the principal floor, with elevations of the entrance and garden fronts, of a large country house to be built in the shape of the letter D. The entrance front flat, with a suite of five rooms in a straight line; the garden front curved, accommodating circular, oval and multi-apsed rooms set round a central oval staircase, expressed as a shallow dome on the exterior. Two-storey colonnaded loggias alternate with single-bay pedimented sections along the curved front.

Small-scale drawings. Originally three sheets. Vol. 46, nos. 106–08. *Insc. Unknown*. The plan and front elevation have a lightly sketched pencil addition of a sweeping carriage way and steps: these are not shown here. The use of rooms, indicated by the design plan in vol. 34, no. 27, is as follows:

A	Hall	F	Mr. Mure's room
B	Dining-room	G	Library
C	Ante-room	H	Dressing-room
D	Drawing-room	I	Principal bedroom
E	Breakfast room		

The frontage extends 138 ft.
Original scale 1 in. to 25 ft.: here 10 mm. to 10 ft.

Great Saxham Hall, an early seventeenth-century house, was altered to designs of Adam in 1774 and destroyed by fire in 1779. Adam prepared three sets of designs for a new building to take its place, though the hall was not to be rebuilt until 1797 and then under the superintendence of Joseph Patience, the younger. Adam's schemes proposed (i) a Palladian house in the manner of Sir Robert Taylor with a central pediment and overlapping lower half pediments to the outer bays of the main block (vol. 34, nos. 13 and 16–22); (ii) a large square house with cruciform wings and many tripartite windows (vol. 34, nos. 28–31) and (iii) the present design (vol. 34, nos. 24–27). A domed central staircase whose volume rises the whole height of the house is common to all designs. Only the principal floor plan of the D-shaped design is drawn up in detail, though it is likely that this scheme was carried furthest, as the plan in vol. 34, is a fully-sized working drawing with the walls coloured in pale red and yellow to distinguish brick and timber work. Equally this is the only design for Great Saxham which the brothers seem to have wished to publish. Sketch designs of the principle and first floor plans with a free-standing portico are in vol. 1, nos. 36 and 37. The Adam scheme for the Jacobean house is illustrated in John Gage, *The History and Antiquities of Suffolk, Thingoe Hundred* (London, 1838) p. 108, and the house is discussed by Norman Scarfe in *The Proceedings of the Suffolk Institute of Archaeology*, vol. 26, p. 230. Hutchinson Mure was the nephew of Adam's client at Caldwell House (Pls. 36 and 37).

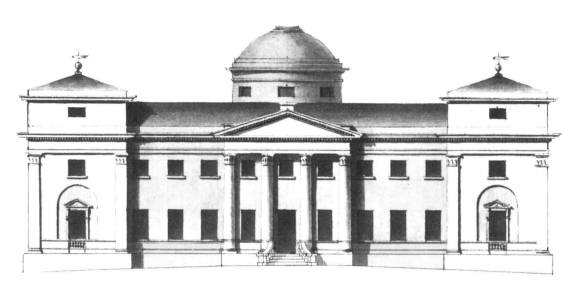

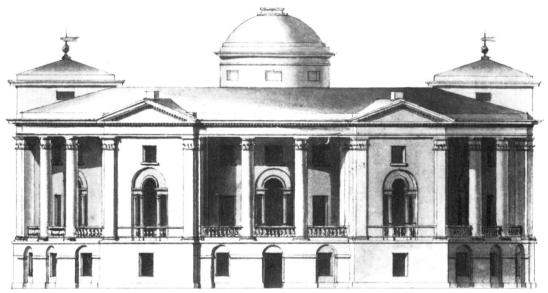

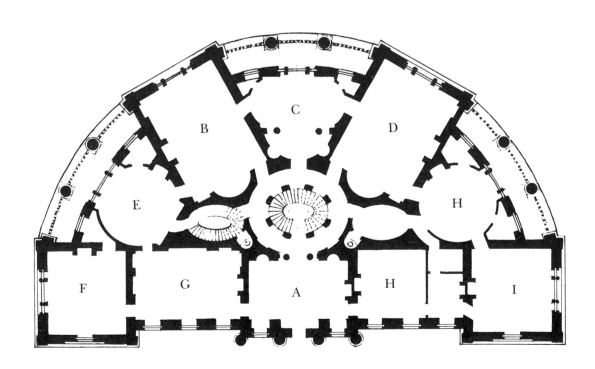

Pl. 13

Plate 14

Design of a small villa on a geometrical plan for a Mr. Wilson.

Plans of the ground floor and principal storey with the front elevation of a fanciful classical trianon containing octagonal, oval and circular rooms with a rectangular hall and stair. The entrance front flat with a shallow loggia and the outer bays canted back.

Large-scale drawings. Originally three sheets, one of elevations and two of plans. Vol. 46, nos. 61–63, reproduced here and Pl. 15. Original dimensions within the borders 420 × 255 mm. *Insc. Principal story of a house for Mr. Wilson* and *Ground story*. Only the principal floor plan is in ink in the original drawings. The use of the rooms is given only for the ground floor.

A	Kitchen	C	Butler's pantry
B	Scullery	D	Men servants' bedroom

The frontage extends 50 ft.
Original scale 1 in. to 10 ft.: here 15 mm. to 10 ft.

Two sketches for this whimsical and intriguing design (vol. 10, nos. 171 and 180) suggest that it may have developed out of a more conventional plan pattern such as Adam adopted in schemes for Sunnyside, near Edinburgh (Pls. 24–28). In these sketches a square hall leads axially into a circular room, with cruciform shaped rooms to left and right. These cruciform rooms are then modified to provide the canted sides of the outer bays on the entrance façade shown here, and a colonnade is added round the circular room on the garden front. In no. 171 Adam proposed a U-shaped stair opening off a square hall on the left, while in No. 180, a diminutive sketch, the stair is triangular.

 The version of the plan prepared for publication is neater and more compact, with the stair occupying part of the hall, thereby releasing the space to the left to be adapted as a shallow octagonal bedroom. Thus in one small area Adam develops a plan of extraordinary complexity in which a circular saloon, an oval dining-room and a polygonal bedroom are grouped round a rectangular hall and staircase and are perfectly interrelated without any waste of space. The hall communicates directly with both public rooms, between which another door allows company to pass from saloon to dining-room without the necessity of returning to the hall. In both these rooms the symmetry of door and window openings is perfectly managed, while in the other parts of the house the domestic arrangements are equally well contrived: Mr. Wilson's bedroom is placed convenient to the stair that leads to the servants' floor below, while the lavatory is located in such a way as to be detached from and yet accessible to, the more public areas of the house.

 Like the much larger D-shaped scheme for Great Saxham Hall, the elevations of this villa contrast not only a flat and a curved front but also, through the device of building the house into the slope of a hill, a wide, low façade on the entrance front and a tall, narrow one on the garden side, where the Bramantean overtones of dome, drum and colonnade are clear. It is the height of this side that is emphasized in an asymmetrical sketch elevation in vol. 1, no. 180. Adam's design for Mr. Wilson's villa offers a striking example both of the fertility of his imagination and the ingenuity of his planning. A similar though ultimately less skilful delight in elaborate plan patterns for villas is reflected in James Peacock's *Oikidia or Nutshells* of 1785.

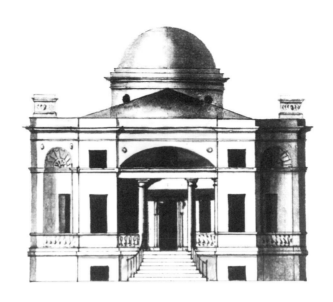

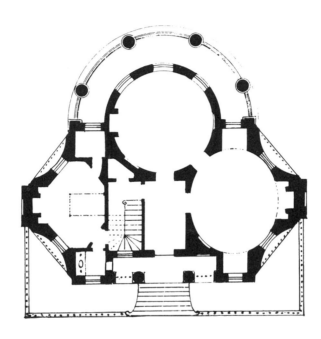

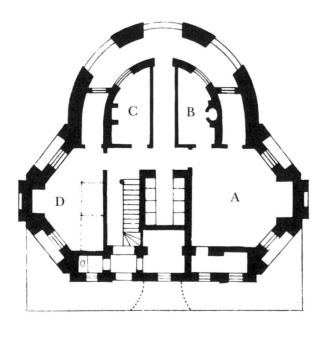

Pl. 14

Plate 15

Design of a small villa on a geometrical plan for a Mr. Wilson.

Plans of the first floor, attics and roof with the rear elevation of a fanciful classical trianon with a semi-circular Roman Doric loggia surmounted by a dome and framed by canted side bays.

Large-scale drawing. Vol. 46, nos. 61 and 63. Original dimensions within the borders 420 × 255 mm. *Insc. House for Mr. Wilson, Bed Chamber Story,* and *Garratts.* The plans reproduced here are pencil outlines in the original. The use of the rooms is not given: all appear to be bedrooms.

The frontage extends 50 ft.
Original scale 1 in. to 10 ft.: here 15 mm. to 10 ft.

The identity of the Mr. Wilson, who commissioned this delightful design is not known. Bolton suggests Sir Thomas Wilson, who subscribed to the Diocletian's Palace volume of 1764, or John Wilson of Pielwall, Berwickshire, who is mentioned in the Political *Report* of 1788 as a man who made his own money and had a small estate. Another voter noted in the *Report* (pp. 21 and 68), also a remote possibility, is James Wilson, a merchant in Kilmarnock, who was living in London and whose affairs were 'deranged' in 1788.

The character of the house recorded here does not seem to be particularly appropriate for any of these gentlemen and a more likely client may be William Wilson (c. 1720–96) of Keythorpe, Leicestershire, whom Robert Adam will have known as a member of the House of Commons, serving in the same Parliament in which the architect sat as member for Kinross. Wilson was a supporter of Lord Bute and was well known to the back-room politician John Robinson, both of whom also employed Adam. He sat as member for Ilchester from 1761 to 1768. In the next parliament he was returned unopposed for Camelford which he represented until 1774. Subsequently two other Adam clients, Sir Samuel Hannay and James Macpherson were elected to represent the borough. Any of these connections might have given rise to patronage by William Wilson of the Adam brothers and there is another argument in his favour. The accommodation provided in the ground floor of this trianon—men servants only—suggests a bachelor establishment. William Wilson was unmarried, a cultured university man, educated at Gray's Inn and Clare College, who, according to Nichols's *History of Leicestershire* (vol. III(1), p. 10) 'passed the principal part of his life at the German Spa and other parts of the Continent and died immensely rich at Pisa in Tuscany' in 1796. The exuberant self-indulgence of this design is nicely calculated for a wealthy, artistic bachelor (Namier & Brooke, vol. 2, p. 647).

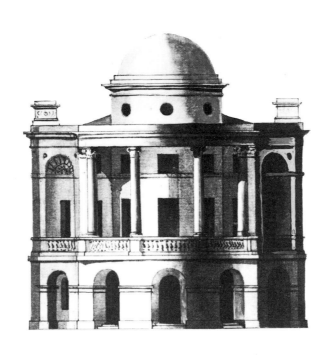

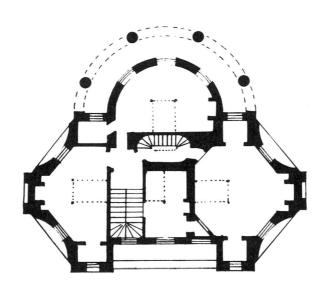

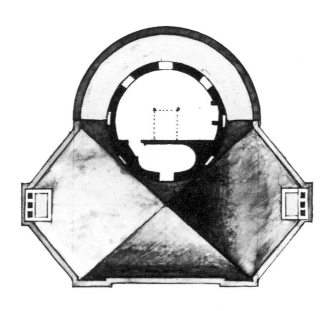

Pl. 15

Plate 16

Design for a new house at Wyke Manor, Isleworth, Middlesex, for John Robinson, M.P.

Elevation of the entrance front with plans of the ground floor and principal storey of a large, three-storey country house to be built on an octagonal plan. In the elevation each angle of the octagon is marked by coupled, giant-order Corinthian columns projecting from the façade, while the accommodation of the interior is arranged as an elaborate sequence of rectangular, semi-circular, oval and multi-apsed rooms set round a central stair.

None of the drawings prepared for engraving in vol. 46 records this design. It is included here for its intrinsic interest as a scheme which the Adam brothers might well have wished to have published had the plans for their last volume been completed. Five drawings for this scheme are preserved in vol. 37, nos. 88–92, including a section and a second-floor plan not reproduced here. The use of the rooms is as follows:

A	Hall	F	Butler	K	Library
B	Great staircase	G	Still room	L	Bedchamber
C	Billiard room	H	Housekeeper	M	Dining-room
D	Steward's room	I	Ante-room	N	Drawing-room
E	Servants' Hall	J	Lady's bedroom		

The frontage extends 88 ft.
Original scale 1½ ins. to 10 ft.: here 10 mm. to 10 ft.

From the autumn of 1778 to November 1779 the Adam office was employed in producing no fewer than four different proposals for a house for John Robinson at Wyke Manor for whom the brothers had also prepared designs for a castle-style villa at Harwich. None of these projects was to be executed, and in the end Adam was called upon to superintend no more than the addition of a two-storey wing to the old house. The ingenious if rather contrived planning recorded in the octagonal scheme is typical of Robert Adam's imagination when operating freely and at an ideal level. He can hardly have expected John Robinson to construct such a monumental design, conceived in the spirit of some inflated belvedere, where the niceties of geometrical repetition provided every room on the first floor with a balcony almost 30 ft. long and numerous not very convenient cupboards, lobbies and recesses on trapezoid and triangular plans. Indeed the centrally planned structure and the division of the elevation, with a giant order to unite the upper floors, evokes memories of James Gibbs's Radcliffe Library at Oxford and carries connotations of a more public architectural character than the suburban villa of any M.P. could support.

The brothers' client at Wyke Manor, John Robinson, was a well-known figure in the House of Commons in the 1770s and 1780s, admired by his contemporaries as a good committee man and reputed to be the member best informed on the opinions of the other members of the house. (Namier & Brooke, vol. II, pp. 364–66). As a successful party manager he will have known Robert Adam while the latter was M.P. for Kinross-shire and also Adam's nephew William, who had a distinguished parliamentary career. In 1773 Robinson quarrelled with his first political patron, Sir James Lowther, also an early patron of Robert Adam, and transferred his interests from Westmorland to East Anglia, where through the Treasury interest he was returned as M.P. for Harwich in 1774. Soon after he purchased Wyke Manor and was planning a villa and town layout at Harwich on property which in its unimproved condition brought in £250 a year.

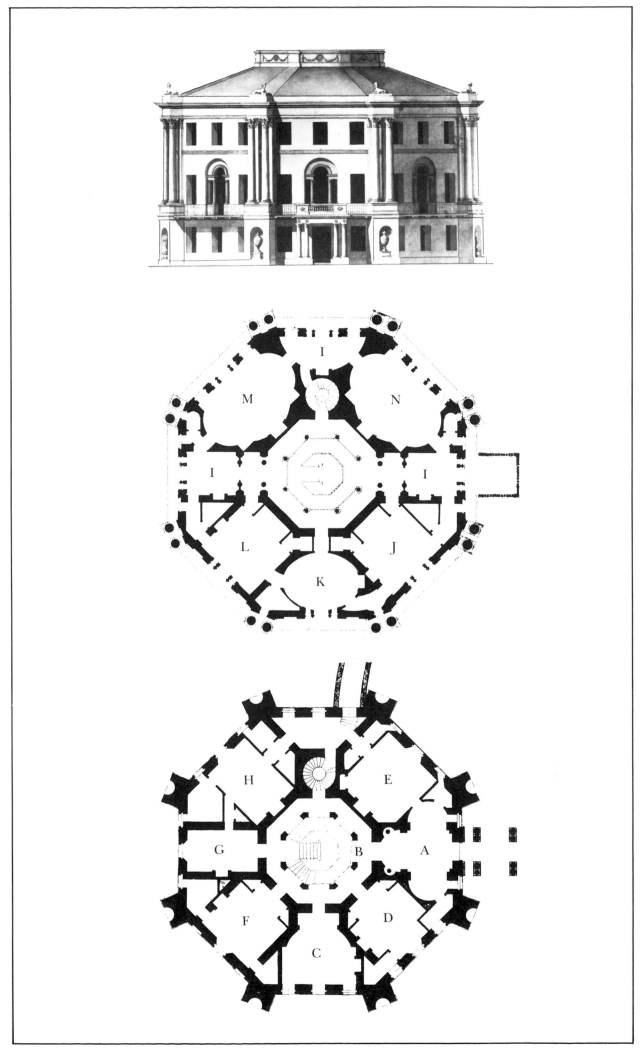

Pl. *16*

Plate 17

Design for Glasserton House, Glasserton, Wigtownshire, for Admiral the Hon. Keith Stewart.

Entrance elevation with ground-floor and first-floor plans of a tall, U-shaped country house with a Tuscan *porte-cochère*, and a central bow on the garden front.

Small-scale drawings. Originally three sheets. Vol. 46, nos. 97, 98 and 99. *Insc. For Honble Keith Stewart*. The use of the ground-floor rooms indicated on the design plan in vol. 45, no. 69, is as follows (no design drawings for the first floor or for the rear elevation are known):

A	Hall	E	Servants' hall	I	Store room
B	Garden parlour or	F	Butler	J	Pantry
	billiard room	G	Housekeeper	K	Kitchen
C	Admiral Stewart's room	H	Female servants	L	Scullery
D	Gun room				

The frontage extends 100 ft.
Original scale 1 in. to 25 ft.: here 10 mm. to 10 ft.

The Adams' scheme for radical alterations to Glasserton is dated 13 November 1787. Though there is no indication on the office design drawings or on the plans prepared for publication that the house was not a new design, its height, the unorthodox appearance of its principal elevation—quite different from the style of other classical compositions by the Adam office at this date—and the unusual shift in scale between the rooms at the front of the house and those at the back all indicate that this was a commission for alterations and not for a new building.

Glasserton, which was demolished in 1950, has a complicated building history and it is not now clear how far the design shown here was carried into execution. In 1883 Groome's *Ordnance Gazetteer of Scotland* describes it as 'a red stone building successor to the seat of the Earls of Galloway which was destroyed by fire in 1730'. No fewer than three architects were involved in its design: John Douglas who prepared a design in 1734, William Adam who made plans in 1737 and John Baxter who altered Douglas's design and built the house between 1739 and 1741. This work was carried out for Alexander, Lord Garlies, eldest son of Lord Galloway who succeeded his father as 6th Earl in 1747. Forty years later, when the Adam brothers were called in, the property had passed to the 6th Earl's third son, the Hon. Keith Stewart (1739–95), who had purchased the barony of Glasserton in 1763 and changed the building's name from Galloway House to Glasserton.

Baxter's house seems to have been old-fashioned and Keith Stewart made several attempts to improve on its layout about 1778 before settling nine years later on the Adam brothers' plan. This proposed a complete rebuilding of the back of the house, with a characteristic bowed saloon in the middle of the façade, and the addition on the entrance front of fore-standing outer bays with a succession of tripartite windows. As built the proportions of the entrance elevation were considerably altered and the central bays under the pediment were executed as three plain windows. A crucial alteration in the Adam scheme was the excavation of the ground in front of the house to reveal the basement and contrive a formal entrance hall at a lower level; this does not appear to have been done.

The Hon. Keith Stewart was M.P. for Wigtown in 1762 and sat for Wigtownshire in 1768 in which year he was appointed receiver-general of the land tax in Scotland. The *Report* of 1788 describes him as having 'a very independent fortune'. He had a distinguished naval career serving under Admiral Keppel in 1778, with Admiral Parker in 1781 and as a Commander with Lord Howe at the relief of Gibraltar in 1782. He was advanced to the rank of rear-admiral in 1790 and vice admiral in 1794. He died at Glasserton on 5 May 1795 aged 56 (*The Scots Peerage*, vol. IV 1907, Earl of Galloway, pp. 165–66).

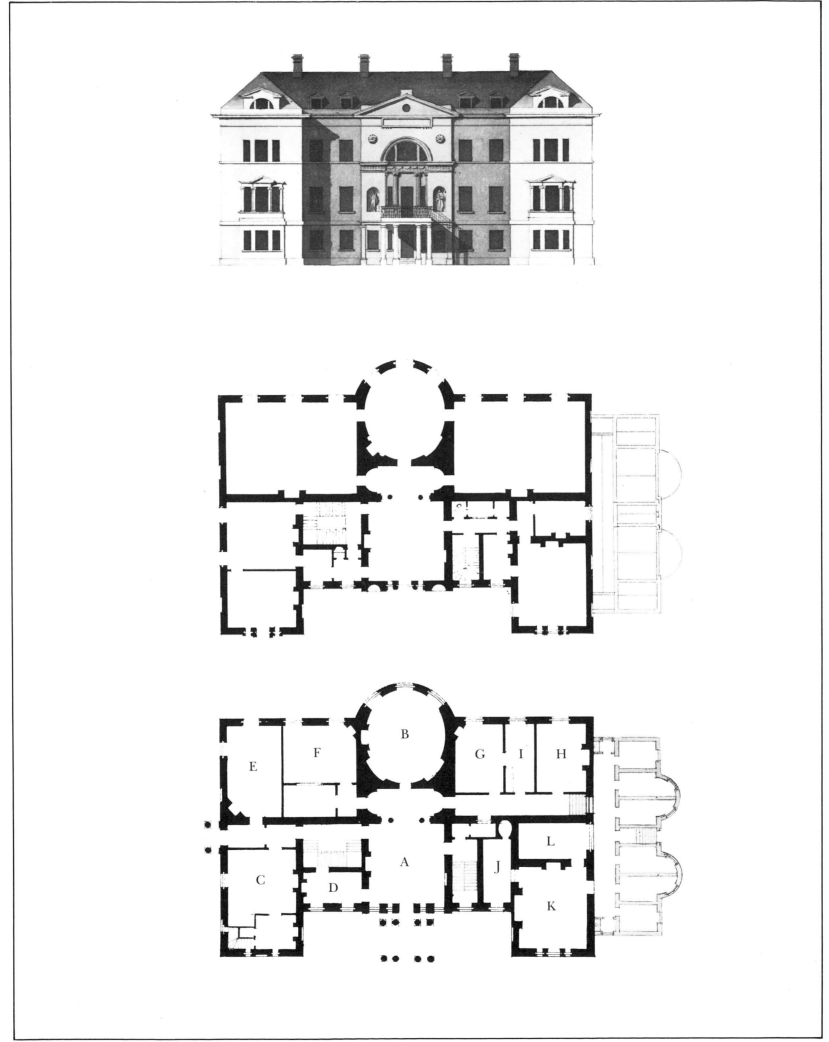

Pl. 17

Plate 18

Design for a new house at The Hill, Putney Heath, for Sir Samuel Hannay Bart., M.P.

Front and rear elevations with ground-floor and first-floor plans of a large rectangular villa. Of three storeys with a Tuscan *porte-cochère* at the front and a bow, in the centre of the rear façade, roofed by an elaborate dome and surrounded by a Tuscan colonnade at ground level.

Small-scale drawings. Originally two sheets, each of a plan and elevation. Vol. 46, nos. 95 and 96. The use of the rooms indicated on the design drawings, vol. 35, nos. 53–61, is as follows:

A	Hall	D	Dining-room
B	Garden parlour	E	Dressing-rooms with powder rooms and w.c.
C	Drawing-room	F	Bedrooms

The frontage extends 78 ft.
Original scale 1 in. to 25 ft.: here 10 mm. to 10 ft.

Three different Adam schemes for The Hill House, Putney, were prepared for Sir Samuel Hannay between 25 October 1786 and some time in 1787. As happened with the brothers' proposals for the suburban residence of another M.P., John Robinson (Pl. 16), the architects' schemes were at first too grandiose, though they ended in modest proposals (vol. 35, nos. 72–74) to add an extra third to the plan of a small square house with a new attic storey built over the top. The design recorded here appears to have been the Adams' second scheme and follows a much larger house (vol. 35, nos. 62 and 63) which was to have had two huge bowed façades fused with a long square block. The outline of this first design seems to envisage a plan similar to that of the oval main block at Ickworth. Even the house shown here was to have provided hot and cold baths in the basement and sixteen bedrooms on two floors. The brothers reduced the decoration to reduce the cost (vol. 35, nos. 70 and 71) ending with a bold astylar scheme, but their client for whom they also designed a country house at Kirkdale in Scotland (Pls. 19, 20 and 21), seems not to have built anything at Putney. Pencil sketches relating to these schemes are in vol. 1, nos. 174 and 203.

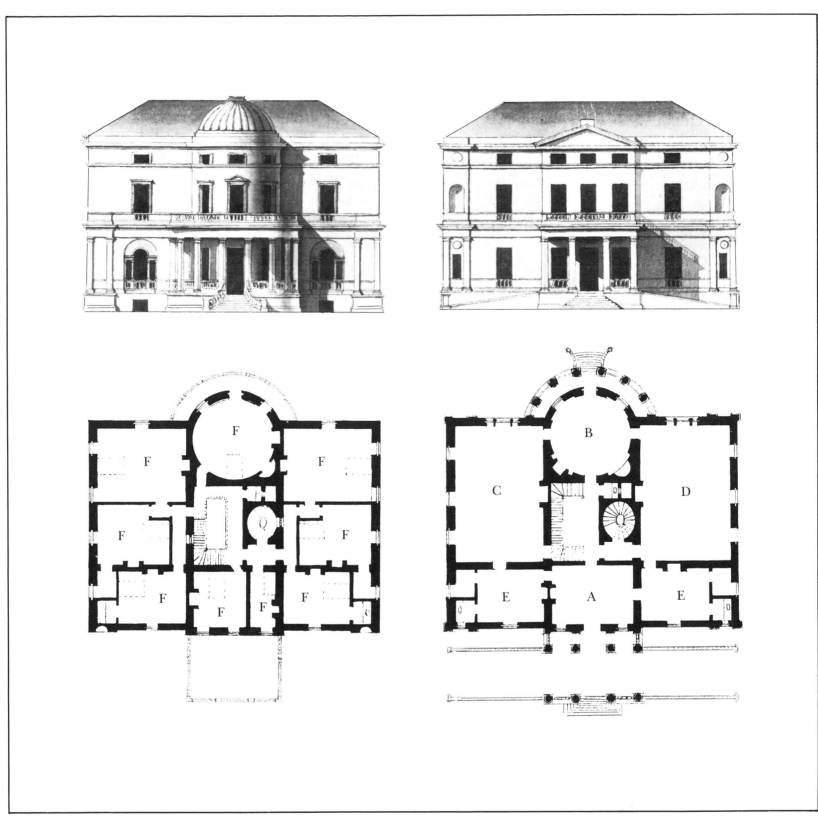

Pl. 18

Plate 19

Designs for Kirkdale House, Creetown, Kirkcudbrightshire, for Sir Samuel Hannay Bart.

Front elevation with the plans of the principal storey and first floor of a large rectangular house with straight wings and square pavilions. A four-columned entrance porch projects between advanced outer bays.

Small-scale drawings. Originally three sheets. Vol. 46, nos. 112, 114 and 116. *Insc. Unknown.* The use of the rooms, as indicated on the design drawings for the larger version of the house shown on Pl. 21 (vol. 35, nos. 32–40), appears to have been as follows:

A	Hall	E	Library
B	Saloon	F	Lobby
C	Dining-room	G	Bedchambers
D	Drawing-room	H	Dressing-rooms

The frontage extends 172 ft.
Original scale 1 in. to 25ft.: here 7.5 mm. to 10 ft.

Sir Samuel Hannay (c. 1742–90), 3rd Baronet of Kirkdale, was one of the Adams' most promising clients in the later 1780s. Had he not died at the age of 48, he might well have employed the brothers for further works in Scotland and in London. Several designs were prepared for his house at The Hill, Putney (Pl. 18), and many more for Kirkdale, the family seat overlooking Wigtown Bay in Galloway including, in addition to the house shown here, elaborate proposals for a complex stable court in the castle style, a cottage, brewhouse and monumental bridge (vol. 35, nos. 32–51, and vol. 51, no. 42). Coloured drawings for the stables are at Blair Adam and in the collection of the Mellon Center for Studies in British Art, Yale University. The obituary notice for Sir Samuel describes him as 'formerly an eminent chemist'. He appears in the London Street Directories as a merchant from 1765 and towards the end of his life was in partnership as a drug merchant with William Duncan. His interests were in the Far East. One brother, Alexander, was a lieutenant-colonel in the Indian army while another, Ramsay, traded from India to China. Sir Samuel himself was wealthy, had important interests in the City and in shipping and was one of the creditors of the Nabob of Arcot whose affairs in Britain were managed by another Adam client, James Macpherson, also an M.P. (Pl. 1). Hannay represented Camelford in the House of Commons from 1784 until his death which occurred on 11 December 1790 (Namier Brooke, vol. II, p. 95).

Kirkdale House was built between 1787 and 1788. Adam designed the bridge for the grounds in November 1788 (vol. 35, no. 49) and the court of castle-style stables in March 1789. The house was damaged by fire in the later nineteenth century and has been reconstructed internally. Its exterior which is executed in finely polished granite ashlar, is however, essentially the same as the smaller design shown here. The stables were built as an octagonal court and not as recorded in the Adam drawings (P. H. McKerlie, *Lands and their owners in Galloway* (Edinburgh, 1878), vol. 4, pp. 255–57).

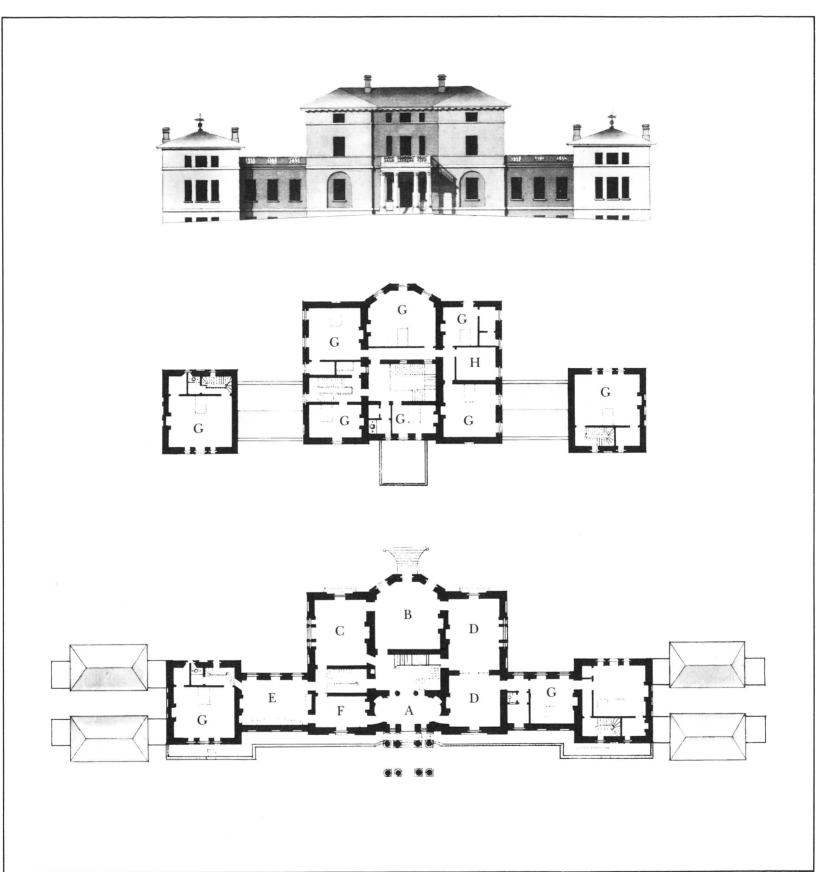

Pl. 19

Plate 20

Designs for Kirkdale House, Creetown, Kirkcudbrightshire,
for Sir Samuel Hannay Bart.

Rear elevation with plans of the ground floor and attics of a large rectangular house with straight wings and square pavilions. Astylar, with a wide canted bay in the centre of the façade.

Small-scale drawings. Originally three sheets. Vol. 46, nos. 111, 113 and 117. *Insc. Unknown.* The use of the rooms, as indicated on the design drawings for the larger version of the house shown on Pl. 21, vol. 35, nos. 32–40, appears to have been as follows:

A	Kitchen	F	Valet's room
B	Butler	G	Beer cellar and larders
C	Housekeeper	H	Servants bedrooms
D	Servants' hall	I	Bedchambers
E	Steward's room		

The frontage extends 172 ft.
Original scale 1 in. to 25 ft.: here 7.5 mm. to 10 ft.

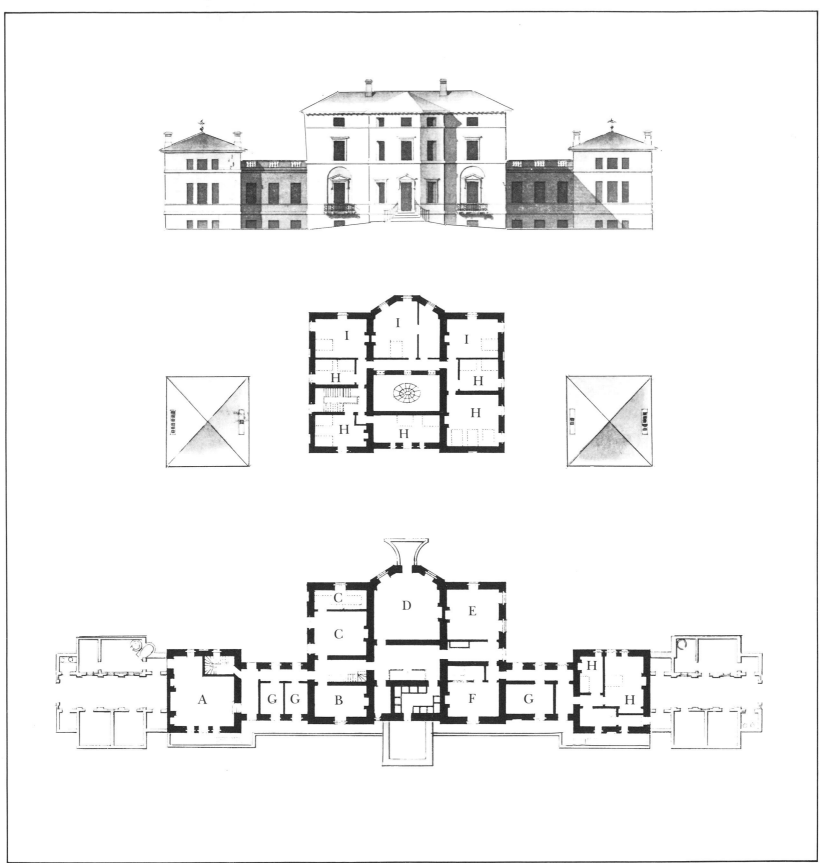

Pl. 20

Plate 21

Designs for Kirkdale House, Creetown, Kirkcudbrightshire,
for Sir Samuel Hannay Bart.

Front and rear elevations of a larger scheme with a longer principal block and more substantial pavilions each with four-eaves pediments. The rear elevation is articulated by an Adam Doric order of pilasters on the upper two floors. Also a section and side elevation of the previous design.

Small-scale drawings. Originally three sheets. Vol. 46, nos. 115, 127 and 128. *Insc. Unknown.*

The frontages extend 198 ft. and 82 ft. on the side elevation.
Original scale 1 in. to 25 ft.: here 7.5 mm. to 10 ft.

A full set of drawings, dating from 1787, records the larger scheme for Kirkdale (vol. 35, nos. 32–40). Like many alternative designs from the Adam office it is closely related to the scheme that was to be built and may be taken to represent a rather more costly version of the same design. One of the design elevations shows an Ionic order as an alternative while a still grander variant proposing an arrangement of coupled Ionic pilasters and an arcaded main floor is recorded in a sketch proposal (vol. 1, no. 222). The tall appearance of the garden front of this scheme may be compared with the second design for Rosebank (Pl. 34) and with the rear elevation of Newliston of 1789 (vol. 32, no. 86; Bolton 1922, chapter 36).

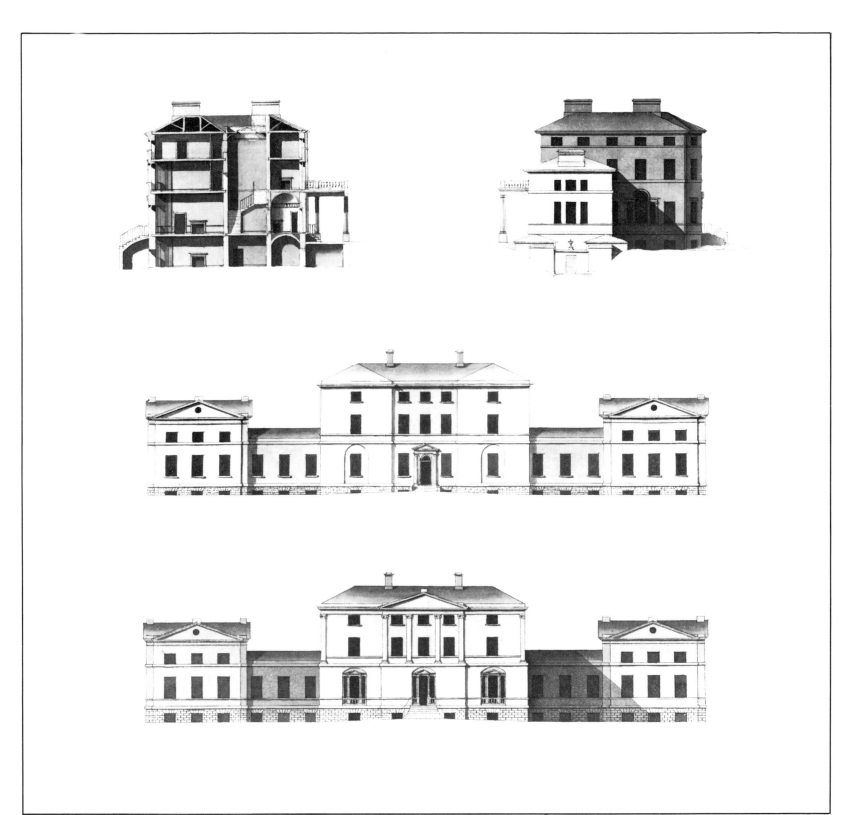

Pl. 21

Plate 22

Design for a rectory at Beckenham, Kent, for the Rev. William Rose.

Front and rear elevations, with basement, ground- and first-floor plans and a section of a plain rectangular house. The entrance front has a single-storey Tuscan *porte-cochère* and there is a canted bay in the middle of the rear façade.

Small-scale drawings. Originally three sheets; two of an elevation and a plan, the third of a section and a plan. Vol. 46, nos. 102–04. A plan of the attic floor, identical to the first floor (no. 105) has been omitted here. The use of the rooms indicated on the design drawings in vol. 35, nos. 101–10, is as follows:

A	Hall	F	Kitchen	K	Dairy
B	Breakfast room	G	Housekeeper	L	Bedchambers
C	Dining-room	H	Washhouse	M	Dressing-rooms
D	Library	I	Butler	N	Powdering-rooms
E	Study	J	Servants' hall		

The frontage extends 52 ft.
Original scale 1 in. to 25 ft.: here 10 mm. to 10 ft.

The design drawings for this austere rectory date from 1788. They follow a more elaborate first proposal which employed a giant order of coupled Ionic pilasters set on a rusticated ground floor. William Rose who was rector of St. George's, Beckenham, from 1778 to 1829 also commissioned designs for picturesque thatched barns and a gate lodge from the Adam brothers (vol. 35, nos. 111–12 and vol. 21, nos. 104 to 106). Sketches relating to these commissions are in vol. 4, nos. 40 and 60, while an intriguing sidelight on the professional rivalry of the Adam office is provided by a slight plan (no. 201 in the same volume) which is inscribed *The Rev^d Mr. Rose's plan by J. Wyatt as sketched by Jo Rose*. In the event neither Wyatt nor the Adams seem to have built a rectory, or anything else, for Mr. Rose.

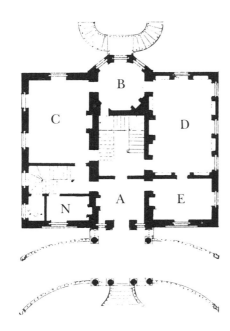

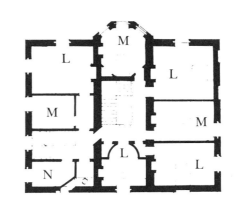

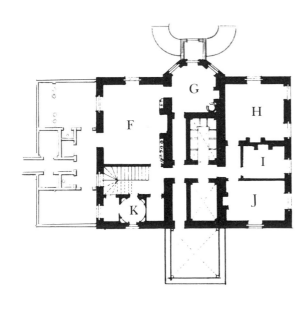

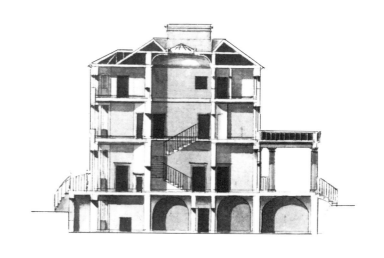

Pl. 22

Plate 23

Design for a small house at Barholm, Creetown, Kirkcudbrightshire, for John McCulloch, Esquire.

Plans of the basement, ground floor and first floor with the front elevation of a small classical villa with a pedimented central block, wings and square pavilions.

None of the drawings prepared for engraving in vol. 46 records this design. It is included here as a representative example of a type of small country house commonly proposed by the Adams and, in this case, built. Seven drawings for the house are preserved in vol. 30, nos. 112–18, including an outline rear elevation, a section and an attic floor plan not reproduced here. The use of the rooms is as follows:

A	Hall	F	Bedrooms
B	Breakfast room	G	Washhouse
C	Drawing-room	H	Housekeeper
D	Dining-room	I	Butler
E	Servants' bedrooms	J	Kitchen

The frontage extends 150 ft.
Original scale 1 in. to 10 ft.: here 10 mm. to 10 ft.

John McCulloch of Barholm, or Balhazy, succeeded to his estate in 1753 and shortly after commissioned a design for a new house which, though it was not built, was included by John Adam as one of the extra illustrations added to *Vitruvius Scoticus* (pl. 94). This early Adam design with a thin central block, straight wings and two pyramid-roofed pavilions provides the starting point for the house shown here. A pencil sketch by Robert Adam, vol. 1, no. 267, dating probably from the summer of 1787 shows that his original intention was to change the wings to quadrants with long rectangular pavilions and walled yards behind, to place the stair to the right of the hall and to add a canted bay window in the middle of the garden front. Of these first proposals only the canted bay at the back of the house remained in the design that was built.

The drawings reproduced here are dated 'Albermarle Street 29 March 1788'. An identical set of client's drawings marked with the sizes and uses of the rooms and a set of working drawings of 9 February 1789 were purchased by the N.M.R.S. Only the main block of the house and the lateral corridors at basement level were built in the architect's lifetime, and Adam does not appear to have supervised the construction of the design. An amateur view by J. Brewis of c. 1836 (N.M.R.S.) shows the centre block with the corridors but no pavilions. About 1850 the left-hand pavilion was built, smaller than Adam intended and in a plain vernacular style. The house was demolished in 1960.

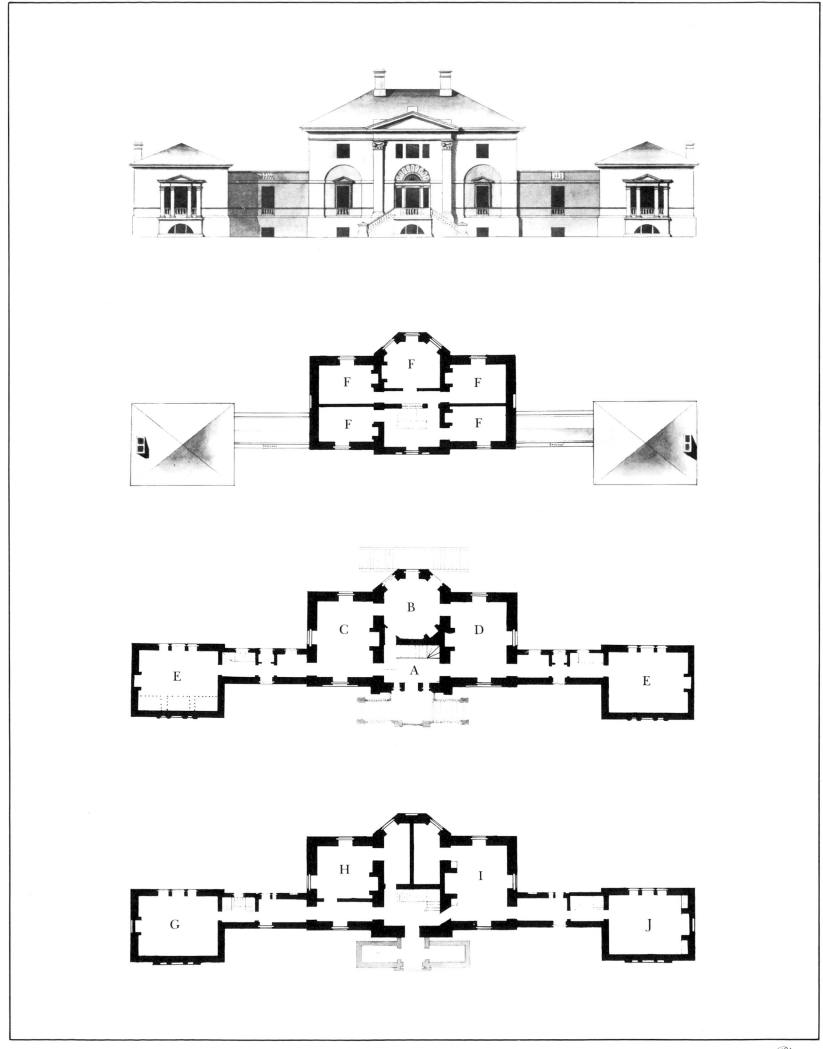

Pl. 23

Plate 24

Design for a suburban villa.

Ground- and first-floor plans with the entrance elevation of a narrow classical villa with a pedimented and domed centrepiece.

Large-scale drawing. Vol. 46, no. 64. Original dimensions within the border 425 × 254 mm. *Insc. Unknown.* The lower plan of the first floor is a modern drawing based on the pencil outline in vol. 1, no. 105. The use of the rooms is not indicated.

The frontage extends 64 ft.
Original scale $\frac{7}{8}$ in. to 10 ft.: here 20 mm. to 10 ft.

The unusual plan of this villa with a narrow entrance hall and staircase, 24 ft. long and 8 ft. wide, set at right angles to the entrance axis, suggests that the design may be linked to Adam's first proposals for a villa for Patrick Inglis at Liberton outside Edinburgh in 1785 (vol. 1, nos. 179 and 180, and vol. 46, nos. 13 and 14). Pencil sketches (vol. 1, no. 169) show that the elevation evolved from a much simpler façade with an eaves pediment in place of the triple arcade with circular lights in the central bays shown here, and plain hipped roofs to the sides of the building instead of the pediments of the present design. The stepped saucer dome with four pediments, the pediments on the side elevations and the projecting bow windows on the ground floor are all lightly added in soft pencil to an otherwise routine little classical façade.

   The genesis of Adam's design for Patrick Inglis's villa, called Sunnyside, is unusually complex, with several designs appearing only to be set aside or modified between 1785 and 1786. The villa itself does not appear to have been begun before 1790 or 1791. The two designs that follow both relate to this commission, though Adam in selecting material for publication may well have considered them as illustrating different concepts and representing separate schemes. Sunnyside, as it was built, is illustrated in Pl. 28. For a particular discussion of these designs see Rowan 1983.

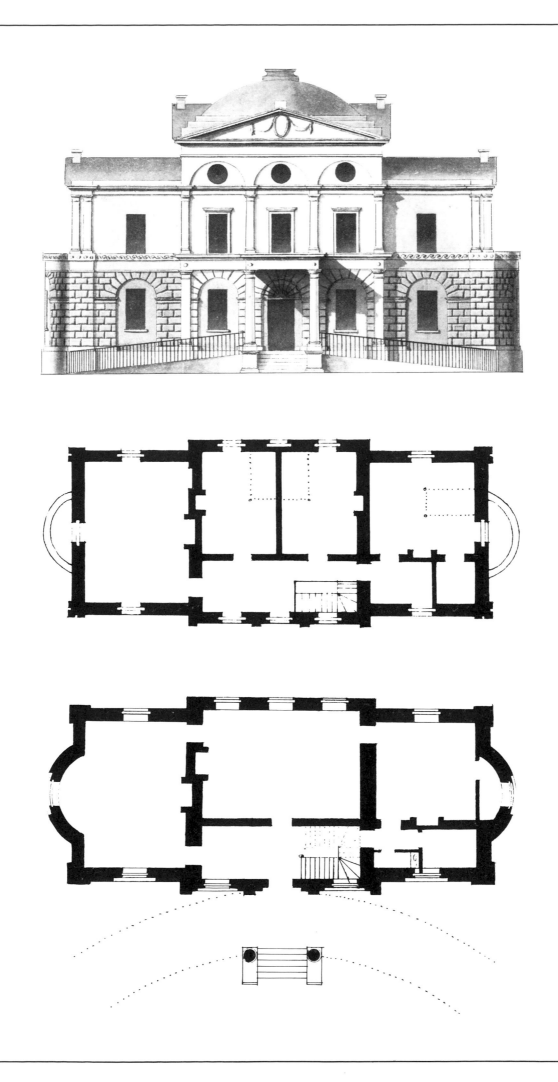

Pl. 24

Plate 25

Design for a suburban villa.

Front and side elevations with the ground-floor plan of a large villa with an entrance loggia recessed between fore-standing blocks and a large reception room with a projecting bay window at the rear.

Large-scale drawing. Vol. 46, no. 69. Original dimensions within the border 425 × 242 mm. *Insc. Unknown.* The use of the rooms indicated on a sketch plan (vol. 1, no. 177) is as follows:

A	Hall	D	Study
B	Drawing-room	E	Book room
C	Eating-room		

The front extends 57 ft. and the side elevation 64 ft.
Original scale $\frac{7}{8}$ ins. to 10 ft.: here 15 mm. to 10 ft.

As with the preceding design, the villa proposed here may be related to Adam's schemes for Patrick Inglis's villa at Liberton near Edinburgh and particularly to two pen sketches (vol. 1, nos. 117 and 257) of a centrally planned structure with a central tower and four Italianate turrets that rise round it. In the present design the turrets have been truncated at eaves level and the central tower, which occupied a position over the staircase and entrance hall and rose between the chimney stacks, has been eliminated. The position of the turrets may be identified on this plan as the two recesses screened by columns in the large room at the back of the house and the two square blocks that flank the entrance loggia. While the plan is a little compromised and not as elegant as it would utimately become, the front that is proposed here has an austere grandeur typical of Robert Adam's late architecture at its very best. A miniature elevation of the Italianate first design is reproduced on p. 23.

A close variant of this scheme (vol. 46, no. 68) seems also to have been prepared for publication though the page was left incomplete. In this version the turret blocks that flank the entrance have been removed and the front is marked by a giant-order, tetrastyle Corinthian portico with a balustraded tower behind it. The effect of this drawing is similar to the principal elevation of the villa designed on a clover-leaf plan (Pls. 26 and 27) to which it closely relates. The drawing is published in Rowan 1983, p. 36.

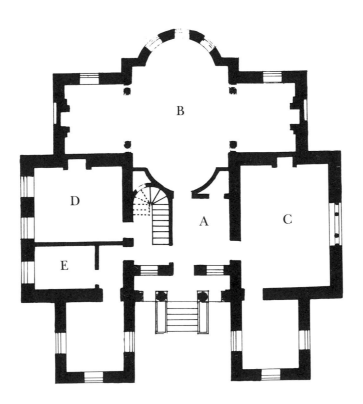

Pl. 25

Plate 26

Design for a villa on a clover-leaf plan.

Principal elevation with the ground-floor and first-floor plans of a classical villa with three bow-fronted rooms arranged round a square stair hall.

Large-scale drawings. Vol. 46, nos. 77 and 79. Originally two sheets with borders measuring 245 × 410 mm. *Insc. Unknown, Plan of the Bed Chamber Story* and *Plan of the Principal Story*. The use of the rooms is as follows:

A	Hall	D	Dressing-room
B	Drawing-room	E	Powder-room
C	Dining-room	F	Bedrooms

The frontage extends 66 ft.
Original scale $\frac{7}{8}$ in. to 10 ft.: here 15 mm. to 10 ft.

As with the preceding two designs the villa shown here may be related to Adam's schemes for Patrick Inglis's villa at Liberton near Edinburgh. This particular design is known only through the finished drawings in vol. 46. The plan with its multiplication of almost identical room shapes, each with a bow on one side, may be compared with a similar example of 'ideal' planning by Adam who prepared a scheme for a house for a Mrs. St. John at Welwyn in Hertfordshire in August 1775 (vol. 45, nos. 17–21) where four such rooms are arranged symmetrically round a square stair hall. It may be noted that the complexity of outline adopted in this plan forced the architect to make use of the eighteenth-century elevational expedient, the dummy window, twelve times on two floors and to devise a quantity of odd cupboards and lobbies on the bedroom floor. In the plan that was finally adopted about 1790 most of these awkward passages had been eliminated.

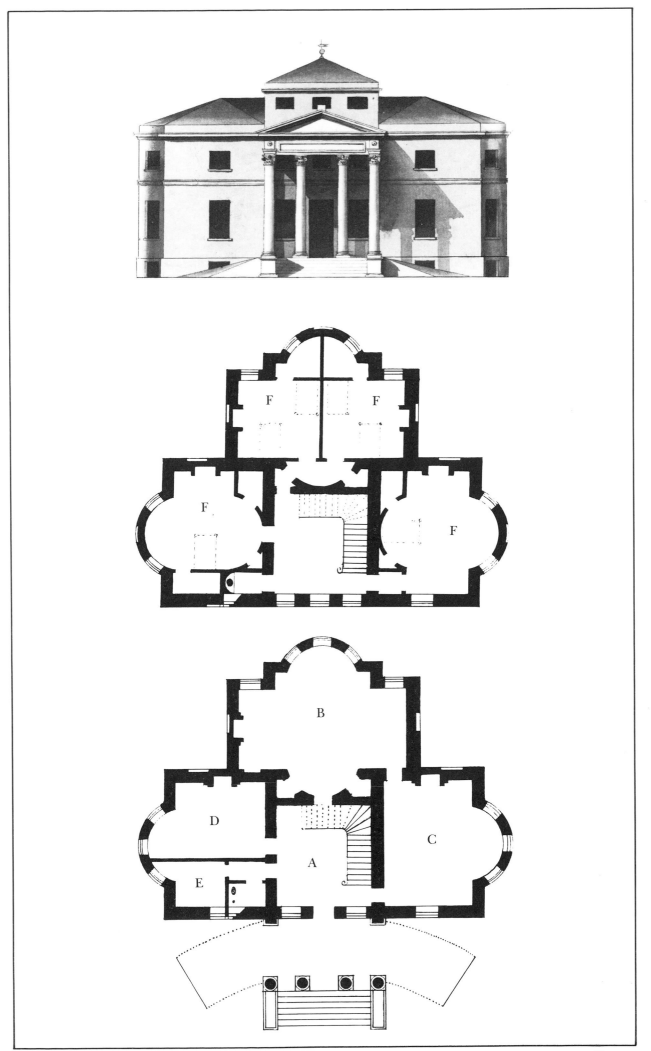

Pl. 26

Plate 27

Design for a villa on a clover-leaf plan.

Rear elevation with the basement and attic floor plans of the preceding design.

Large-scale drawings. Vol. 46, nos. 78 and 80. Originally two sheets with borders measuring 245 × 410 mm. *Insc. Unknown, Plan of the Attick Story* and *Plan of the Ground Story.* Only the kitchen, K, is marked on the plans, though the outline of beds are shown in all the other ground-floor rooms, which seems odd.

The frontage extends 66 ft.
Original scale $\frac{7}{8}$ in. to 10 ft.: here 15 mm. to 10 ft.

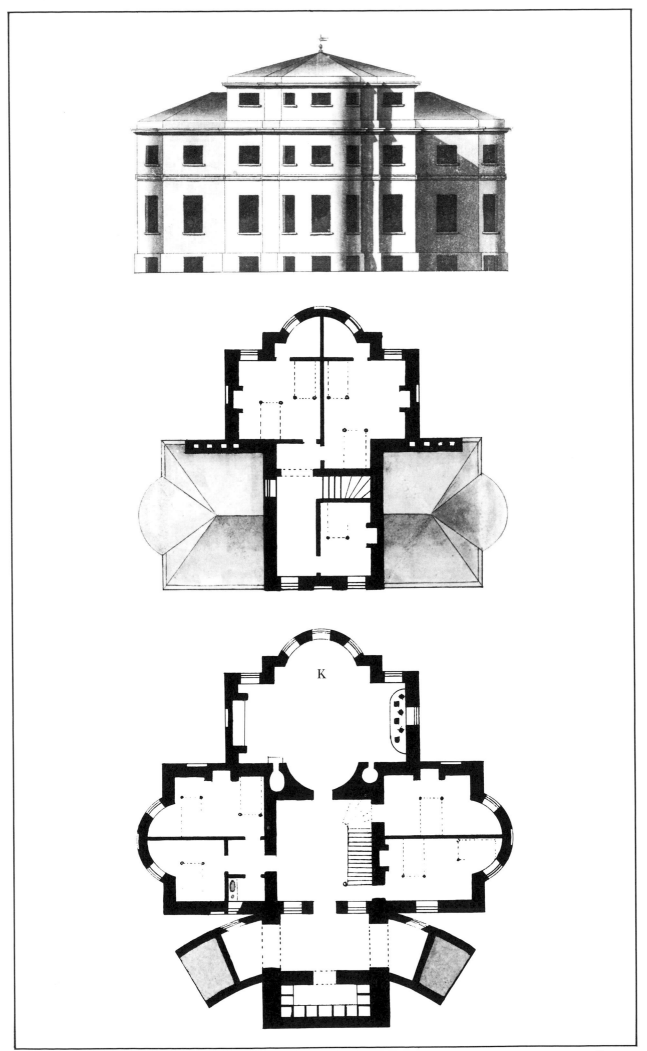

Pl. 27

Plate 28

Design for Sunnyside, Liberton, near Edinburgh, for Sir Patrick Inglis, Bart.

Front and rear elevations with the ground-floor plan of a classical villa: a Tuscan *porte-cochère* set between slightly advanced pedimented blocks on the front; the rear elevation stepped with a central bow.

Drawings for Sunnyside prepared for publication exist both to the large scale (vol. 46, no. 65) and as miniature designs (vol. 46, nos. 118 and 119). Both sets of drawings show the entrance façade and the ground-floor plan and all are inscribed *Unknown*. The large-scale drawing is reproduced here with a modern drawing of the rear elevation added to it. Original dimensions within the border are 425 × 247 mm. The use of the rooms, inscribed on no. 65, is as follows:

A	Hall	C	Dining-room
B	Drawing-room	D	Dressing-room or Study

The frontage extends 62 ft.
Original scale $\frac{3}{4}$ in. to 10 ft.: here 15 mm. to 10 ft.

The earliest drawings relating to Sunnyside date from 1785 and 1786, though as the building is described in 1792 as 'a handsome and elegant house just now rearing up' it may not have been begun before 1790 or 1791. A comparison of the plan of Sunnyside with the preceding three schemes demonstrates how Adam's design sharpened during the year in which he experimented with different ideas for the house. In its final appearance the entrance front is one of the most controlled of Adam's elevations, balanced and scrupulously integrated by a limited number of carefully positioned motifs.

The brothers' draughtsmen tended to treat minor details with some freedom, and the different schemes for this front—the large one probably drawn in Albemarle Street, London, and the small one in Edinburgh—record slight differences in the two façades. The smaller drawing raises the level of the roof, omits the chimneys, flattens the pitch of the pediments and omits, perhaps because it is to a smaller scale, the architrave and console brackets on the first floor windows in the outer bays. As the front of the house was totally obscured by the addition of a new manorial-style range in about 1850, the original appearance of Sunnyside cannot now be know. It is however possible that the Edinburgh draughtsman gave the truer record; portions of the house that survive today show a rather bald rear elevation and projecting side bays that lack the roof pediments recorded in this design. The building is now a golf club.

A connection exists between Robert and James Adam and their client at Sunnyside, Patrick Inglis of Craigs. Inglis was an Edinburgh merchant, the fifth son of Sir John Inglis of Cramond, 2nd Bart., from whom he ultimately inherited the baronetcy. His first cousin was John Clerk of Eldin who was married to Susan Adam, and it was their daughter Susan who was largely responsible for taking care of and ordering the collection of her uncles' architectural drawings. The pedigree of the Inglis family extracted from Douglas's *Baronage of Scotland* is reproduced in John Philip Wood, *The Parish of Cramond* (Edinburgh, John Paterson, 1794), p. 265.

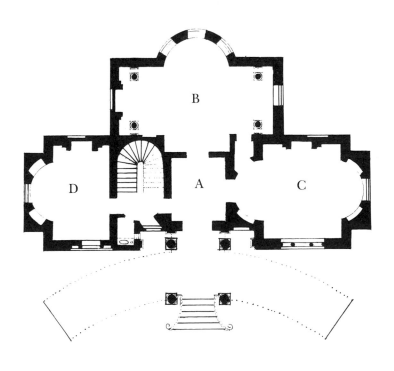

Pl. 28

Plate 29

Design for a new house at Congalton, near North Berwick, East Lothian, for William Grant, Esquire.

Front and rear elevations with the ground- and first-floor plans of a small country house with a pedimented central block, wings and square pavilions.

Small-scale drawing. Only the drawing of the entrance front, vol. 46, no. 129, partially rendered in wash (and here completed), is preserved among the designs prepared for publication. The rear elevation is a modern drawing and the plans are taken from the office designs in vol. 45, nos. 81–83. The elevation in vol. 46 is inscribed *Unknown*. The use of the rooms is as follows:

A	Hall	D	Dining-room
B	Drawing-room	E	Bedchambers
C	Breakfast room	F	Dressing-rooms

The frontage extends 150 ft.
Original scale 1 in. to 25 ft.: here 10 mm. to 10 ft.

The office drawings for Congalton are dated 30 April 1790 and were prepared in Albemarle Street, London. They are described as 'A New Design' though no other scheme for this property is known. The drawings must have been taken to Scotland by Robert when he made his annual visit later that year, no. 81 is endorsed on the back 'from Edin[b]. 22 July 1796', which can only refer to Mrs. Drysdale's action in sending the contents of the Edinburgh office down to London after Robert and James's deaths (see Introduction p. 11). This commission was unusual in so far as William Grant, for whom the design was made, was not the proprietor of Congalton, though he apparently contemplated purchasing it from the Hepburn Congalton family whose last member died in 1804. The property is listed in the Ordnance Survey Name Book of 1853 as 'a small house and outhouses' having about nine or ten acres of land. It had descended from the Hepburn Congaltons to the family of Lord Clinton, from which it would appear that William Grant never made his purchase and had in consequence no opportunity to build the Adam house.

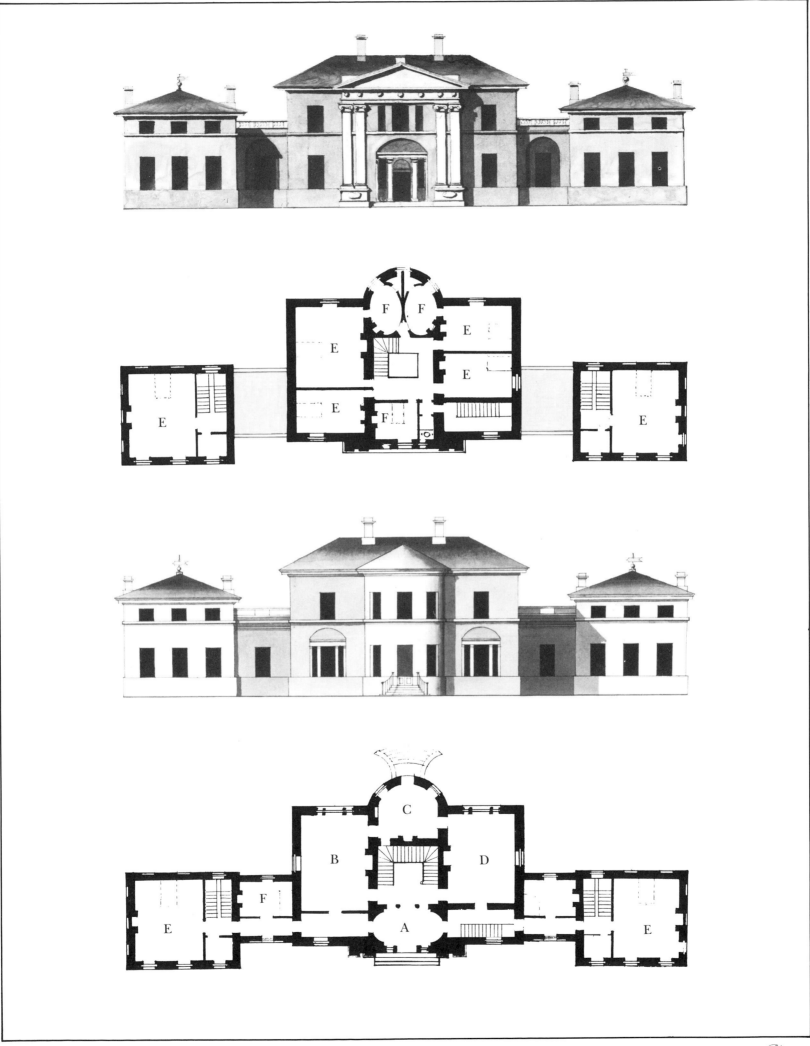

Pl. 29

Plate 30

Design for additions to Wyreside Hall, Cockerham, Lancashire, for John Fenton Cawthorn Esquire, M.P.

Ground-floor plan and two elevations of a scheme for elaborate classical additions with a pedimented central block and domed pavilions to be added across the end of an older house.

Small-scale drawings. Originally two sheets. Vol. 46, nos. 109 and 110. *Insc. Unknown.* The use of the rooms indicated on a design plan (vol. 36, no. 100) is as follows:

A	Hall	E	Mr. Cawthorn's room	H	Dressing-room
B	Eating-room	F	Court	I	Powder-room
C	Parlour	G	Bedchamber	J	Stables
D	Drawing-room				

The frontages extend 77 and 128 ft.
Original scale 1 in. to 25 ft.: here 10 mm. to 10 ft.

The alterations proposed for Wyreside Hall consisted of two ranges to be built in the shape of an L across the southwest end of an earlier house. Two schemes were prepared. One in the castle style (vol. 36, no. 99) proposes a principal block of the same proportions as the classical scheme, though given square towers at the corners, low battlemented walls to screen the courts, and terminal pavilions with central round towers in place of the domed square blocks of the classical scheme. Three elevations, now in the Victoria and Albert Museum (nos. 3328–3330), show that the brothers also proposed a variant of the scheme illustrated here in which the domed pavilion blocks were given pediments like those in Pl. 24 and the height of the outer bays of the main block was reduced.

The office copy of the main floor (vol. 36, no. 100) is the only working plan for this house that survives. Formerly dated, it now reads '5 June 179–' with the last numeral excised. The plan is in two colours showing the longer west front in black as already executed and the short façade in pink as a proposed addition or more probably a remodelling to make the south front of the house accord with the shorter elevation shown here. At this time tripartite windows were to be set into the corner pavilions and the Tuscan porch was to be built in the middle of the west front. It would appear therefore that the job, like a number of Adam commissions at this time, was carried out in stages and that the first addition, the west front, was built probably in the late 1780s. Pencil sketches related to this design are in vol. 1, nos. 50 and 185.

John Fenton Cawthorn (1753–1831) was M.P. for Lincoln from 1783 to 2 May 1796 and for Lancaster intermittently from 1806 until his death. His introduction to the Adam brothers came however not through parliament, nor through his development of improved farming methods at Wyreside—an interest that he shared with James Adam—but through his father-in-law, Lord Delaval, for whom the brothers had designed Milburn, at Claremont in Surrey in 1786 (see Pl. 5). Fenton Cawthorn had married Frances Delaval in 1778, and it was perhaps his wife as much as he who wanted to make the old house more up-to-date. Either the costs of Adam's architecture or the expenses of improvement farming led to financial disaster, however, as Cawthorn was expelled from parliament for embezzlement in 1796. The building work at that time had to be halted and was not resumed. Wyreside is the subject of a long notice in *The Lonsdale Magazine or Provincial Repository*, no. XVIII (June 1821), which includes a view of the house showing the centre of the west front completed according to the Adams' designs, though an older house remains at the southern end where one of the domed pavilions should have been. In 1836 the property was sold to Robert Garnett who seven years later rebuilt the house in a plain classical manner and on a plan that still clearly reflects the influence of the Adam elevational scheme.

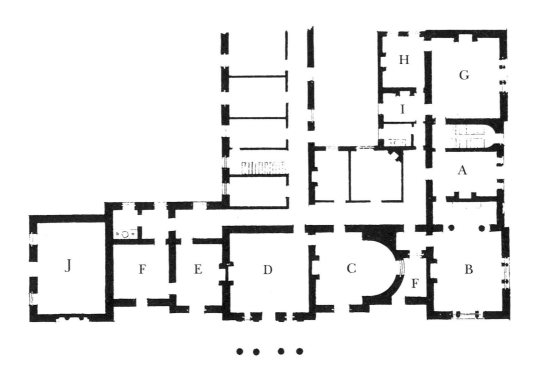

Pl.   30

Plate 31

Design for a villa with a pyramid roof.

Front elevation with the ground- and first-floor plans of a rectangular villa with corridor wings and pedimented square pavilions.

Large-scale drawings. Originally three sheets. Vol. 46, nos. 71, 74 and 75. Dimensions within the border 272 × 448 mm. and 217 × 453 mm. *Insc. Unknown, Principal Story* and *Bed Chamber story*. The use of the rooms is not given.

The frontage extends 134 ft.
Original scale 1 in. to 10 ft.: here 15 mm. to 10 ft.

Six highly finished design drawings record this anonymous villa whose development is also represented by pencil sketches in vol. 1 and by less finished variant designs in vol. 46. The state of finish of the drawings reproduced here seems to suggest that the scheme was regarded in the Adam office as in some way definitive, though the layout of the individual sheets and their size does not accord with that of any of the other designs prepared for publication.

Among the pencil sketches the sequence of designs from which this elevation develops, all in vol. 1, is nos. 269, 196 and 206, where the last sketch is close to the finished entrance front, differing only in the provision of splayed steps with fan-lit doors in the centre of the pavilions and the addition of sphinxes at the base of the main steps. A more remote variant which develops from the pylon-like façade of this design, and from the juxtaposition of the straight main stair and spiral secondary stair, is represented by two other villa designs partially washed in but not sufficiently developed or finished to seem possible as candidates for inclusion in any book of designs. These are vol. 46, nos. 87–89 (which may be compared with sketches in vol. 1, nos. 108, 133 and 137, and vol. 10, nos. 46 and 131) and vol. 46, no. 67, which relates to further sketches in vol. 1, nos. 104, 121 and 229 and vol. 10, no. 130. A degree of overlap exists between both of these design types and the pyramid-roofed villa illustrated here.

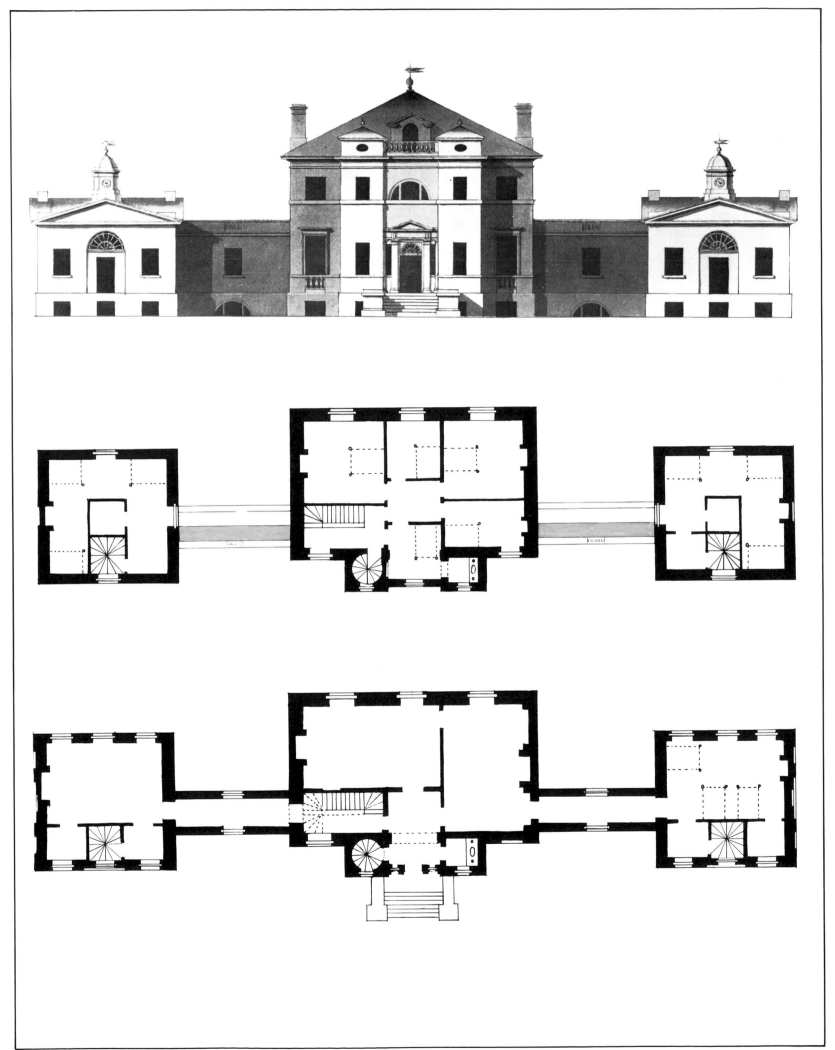

Pl. 31

Plate 32

Design for a villa with a pyramid roof.

Rear elevation with the basement and attic floor plans of the preceding design.

Large-scale drawings. Originally three sheets. Vol. 49, nos. 72, 73 and 76. Dimensions within the border 272 × 448 mm. and 217 × 453 mm. *Insc. Unknown, Garrett Story* and *Ground Story to the foregoing.* The use of the rooms is not given.

The frontage extends 134 ft.
Original scale 1 in. to 10 ft.: here 15 mm. to 10 ft.

The astylar rear elevation and pyramid roof of the main block in this villa also occur in two late Adam projects to which this design may be related. The closest similarity is with the rear elevation of the main block of Linthouse near Govan designed for James Sproule in December 1791 (vol. 31, nos. 91–96). Woodburn House, Dalkeith, designed for James Kerr in February 1792 (vol. 33, nos. 97–101), seems to have employed a similar rear elevation. The very considerable quantity of rough sketches that have been preserved and which record Adam's first thoughts on this scheme would support a late date for its design.

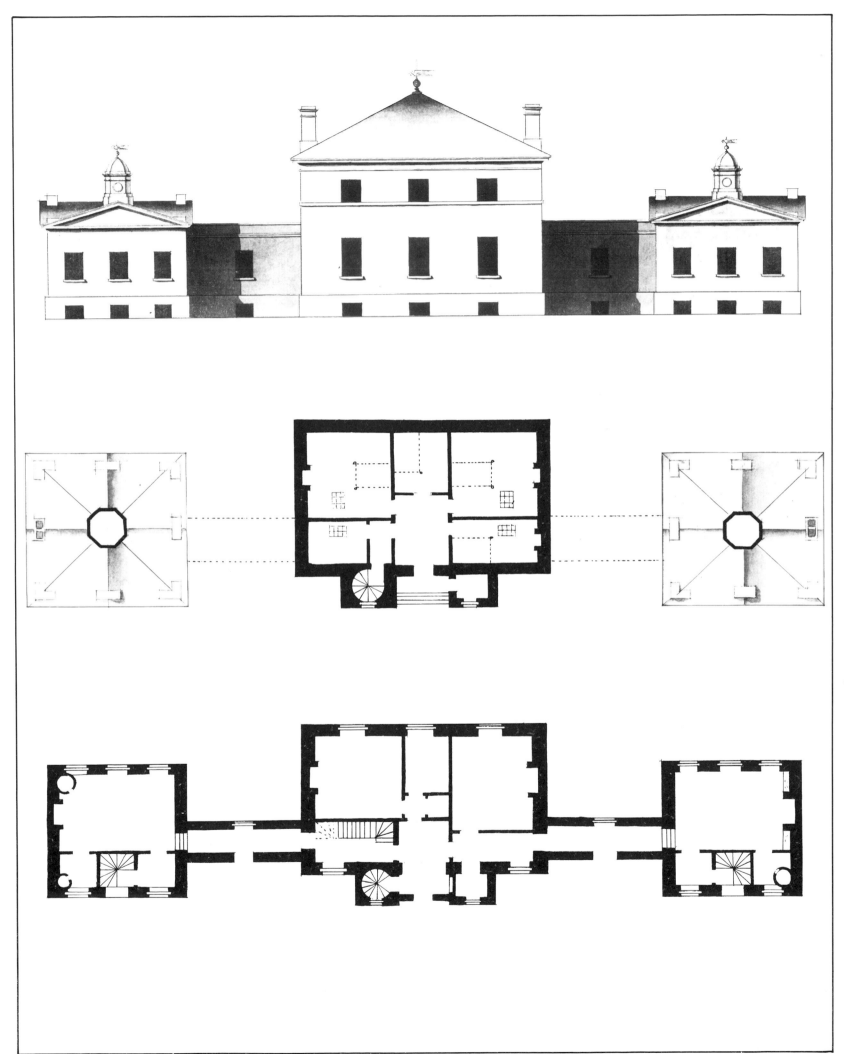

Pl. 32

Plate 33

Design for a house at Rosebank, Cambuslang, Lanarkshire, for John Dunlop, Esquire.

Front and rear elevations with plans of the basement, ground floor, first floor and attics of a tall classical house. The entrance front with a rusticated ground floor supporting a giant order of Ionic columns and pilasters; the rear with paired segmental bows.

Small-scale drawings. Originally five sheets. Vol. 46, nos. 121–26. *Insc. Unknown.* The ground-floor plan is taken from a design drawing, vol. 30, no. 56. The use of the rooms as indicated in a sketch plan, of the ground floor and first floor only, vol. 1, no. 120, is as follows:

A	Eating-room	E	Library
B	Ante-room	F	Dressing-room
C	Drawing-room	G	Family bedroom
D	Butler	H	Parlour or Study

The frontage extends 84 ft.
Original scale 1 in. to 25 ft.: here 10 mm. to 10 ft.

Adam's first proposal for Rosebank, for which three alternative façades were designed in 1789, was to add a new range of building across the front of an older house. Though it is not dated, the scheme illustrated here is inscribed '2nd Design for a House for John Dunlop Esq.' and seems to relate in its formal elements more to town architecture such as Adam's work at Charlotte Square, Edinburgh, or his proposals for Stirling Square in Glasgow than to villa design.

The brothers' client at Rosebank, John Dunlop, was a well-known and wealthy Glasgow merchant who in 1794 became Lord Provost of the city. He had inherited the estate of Rosebank, picturesquely situated near the Clyde, through his wife. Though Dunlop was anxious to develop this property, after the deaths of the Adams he seems to have lost interest in the idea. The estate was sold in 1801 to the cotton manufacturer David Dale still in an unimproved state.

Adam's other designs for this house are discussed in Rowan 1983. For Dunlop see *D.N.B.*

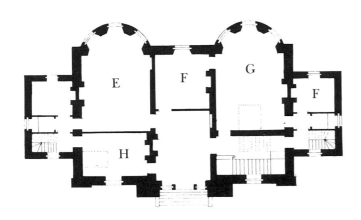

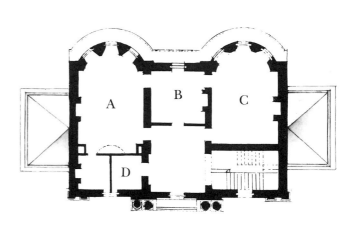

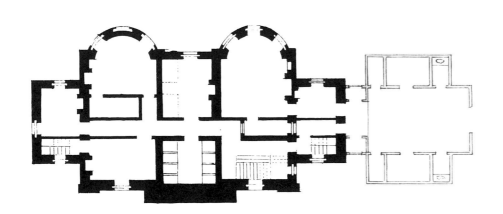

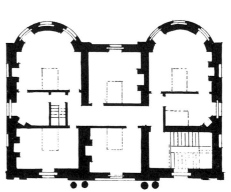

Pl. 33

Plate 34

A second design for a house at Rosebank, Cambuslang, Lanarkshire, for John Dunlop, Esquire.

Front and rear elevations with plans of the basement, ground floor, first floor and attics of a rectangular house with wings and square pavilions. The entrance front with a rusticated ground floor and pedimented centrepiece supported by coupled Ionic half-columns; the rear with a central bow and pilasters at the corners of the main block.

There are no drawings among the designs prepared for publication in vol. 46 which record this scheme for Rosebank. The various alternative designs which were drawn up for Kirkdale and Sunnyside suggest that the Adams intended to publish more than one version of some commissions, and this scheme for Rosebank is sufficiently different from the preceding plate to suggest that it might well have had a place in the brothers' book. Seven drawings for this project, vol. 30, nos. 48–51, include a section which is not reproduced here. *Insc.* variously *Elevation* or *Plan of a New Design for John Dunlop Esq.* The use of the main rooms is as follows:

A	Hall	E	Book room	H	Bedchambers
B	Study	F	Family bedroom	I	Dressing-rooms
C	Drawing-room	G	Kitchen	J	Servants' bedroom
D	Eating-room				

The frontage extends 134 ft.
Original scale 1 in. to 10 ft.: here 10 mm. to 10 ft.

The scheme recorded here is one of Robert Adam's last designs. Earlier proposals for Rosebank date from February 1789. These drawings signed by Adam are dated to 1792, within two months of his death. A pencil sketch of the main façade is in vol. 1, no. 208. Adam's account book of his last visit to Scotland records a meeting with Dunlop at Rosebank on 14 September 1791 when the two men dined afterwards at Carmyle (Sanderson 1982, pp. 35–45). This final version of the brothers' design for a villa was no doubt an outcome of the discussions held then.

Pl. 34

Plate 35

Design for Walkinshaw, Barrhead, Renfrewshire for Dayhort Macdowall, Esquire.

Front and side elevations with the ground- and first-floor plans and a section of a large triangular villa. Astylar with an octagonal tower and attic storey at each corner.

There are no drawings for Walkinshaw among the designs prepared for publication in vol. 46. The house is included here as representing one of the most perfect solutions, in an ideal sense, to the problem of villa design. The drawings reproduced are from vol. 31, nos. 56–63, excluding the basement and attic plans. *Insc. South front of a New Design for Walkinshaw for Dayhort Macdowall Esquire, Plan of the Principal Story, Section* etc. The front elevation is signed *Robt. Adam Archt. 1791.* The railings shown on this front and the back stairs in the section are a modern redrawing. The use of the rooms is as follows:

A	Hall	E	Drawing-room
B	Study	F	Bedchambers
C	Eating-room	G	Dressing-rooms
D	Breakfast room	H	Powder room

The longer frontage extends 85 ft.: the shorter 65 ft.
Original scale $\frac{3}{4}$ in. to 10 ft.: here 10 mm. to 10 ft.

As a basis for architectural fantasies, or for light-hearted garden buildings, triangular plans appear regularly in British eighteenth-century architecture and in architectural publications. Two features distinguish Adam's design at Walkinshaw from those of his contemporaries: its scale—it is a full-sized country house—and the fact that it is based on a broad isosceles triangle rather than the more common equilateral form. This has clear advantages in the plan: for example, the two rear (or side) elevations of the house meet at right angles which permits the architecture to develop rationally along two fronts so that the internal planning of the house is not sacrificed to an external architectural ideal. Indeed the plan of the house, like the villa for Mr. Wilson (Pls. 14 and 15), succeeds in eliminating circulation space almost entirely and works well on the first floor, where five good bedrooms are each supplied with sensibly shaped rectangular dressing-rooms in a convenient plan. It is only in the lighting of these dressing-rooms that the architecture becomes contrived. A source for the plan of Walkinshaw may be identified in a sketch for a small triangular castle, vol. 10, no. 23, while an outline of the bedroom floor plan and a side elevation are in vol. 1, nos. 48 and 75. Triangular and other geometric designs by the Adam brothers are discussed in Rowan 1974d, pp. 695–709.

In the summer and late autumn of 1791, Robert Adam made three visits to Glasgow and the surrounding district. On the first of these, about mid-July 1791, he visited Castle Semple in Renfrewshire whose owner, William Macdowall of Garthland, had asked him to prepare designs to convert a Scottish Palladian house into an Adam castle (vol. 30, nos. 79 and 80). Nothing came of this, but Adam was also engaged to prepare designs for Mr. Macdowall's third son Dayhort (1753–1809), who was to be married in November that year and who intended to build a new house at Walkinshaw for himself and his bride. Adam's drawings for Walkinshaw were designed in the Edinburgh office that summer and the house had presumably already been begun when the architect visited the site on 17 September. The circular windows shown in the attic of the entrance front were changed in execution to normal square-headed sashes. Though no other triangular house by Adam exists it is worth noting that the alterations of 1807 to Airth Castle, Stirlingshire, carried out by David Hamilton of Glasgow converted that house to a triangular plan and that Dayhort Macdowall's wife, Wilhelmina Graham, came from Airth Castle (see J. P. Neale, *Views of Seats*, series 2, vol. 3 (1826), and *Burke's Landed Gentry* (1894)). Walkinshaw is noticed in A. H. Millar, *Castles and Mansions of Renfrewshire and Bute* (1889). The house was demolished about 1927.

Pl. 35

Plate 36

Design in the castle style for Caldwell House, Beith, Ayrshire, for Baron Mure of Caldwell.

Front elevation with the ground- and first-floor plans of a rectangular house, with battlemented parapets and angle bartizans.

There are no drawings for this commission among the designs prepared for publication in vol. 46. The drawings reproduced here (and in Plate 37) are taken from a set of finished design drawings in the Scottish Record Office (RHP 2549). The use of the rooms, indicated in the office copy drawings (vol. 37, nos. 70–77), is as follows:

A	Hall	F	Mrs. Mure's bedchamber
B	Breakfast room	G	Mrs. Mure's dressing-room
C	Dining-room	H	Bedchambers
D	Drawing-room	I	Dressing-rooms
E	Library	J	Powdering-room

The frontage extends 119 ft.
Original scale approximately 2 in. to 15 ft.: here 9 mm. to 10 ft.

The decision to build Caldwell in the castle style was taken late in the evolution of the design. The first proposals are for an elaborate neo-classical scheme (vol. 42, nos. 14 and 15), with a large bow in the centre of the entrance front, surrounded by free-standing columns of a giant order, paired bows on the garden front and a complex interior plan. This scheme was succeeded by 'a New Design for Mr. Baron Mure at Caldwell' dated 25 Nov 1771 (vol. 42, nos. 7–13) which establishes the plan of the house as published here but envisages classical elevations in which the central block on each front is articulated by paired Ionic pilasters of an Adam type. The wide spacing of the windows on the main front was well adapted to such an elevational treatment and, when the house became a castle, left a legacy of blankness that is not entirely resolved by the tall yet essentially shallow relieving arches drawn across the façade.

Built in 1773, Caldwell is one of the last examples of the Adam brothers' early castle manner of which Ugbrooke in Devon (1763), Whitehaven Castle in Northumberland (1768) and Mellerstain in Berwickshire (1770) are earlier and larger examples. Features here, which are typical of the early castles generally, are the regular succession of square-headed windows with label mouldings above them, the flatness of the façades and the rectangular, boxy appearance of the overall design. While these elements largely disappear from later castle schemes, the unusual 'machicolated cornice', which Adam sets immediately below the battlements, and the circular bartizans at each corner of the wall-head appear first at Caldwell and soon become standard motifs of the castle style.

Robert and James Adam probably owed their introduction to William Mure of Caldwell through their contacts with the Earl of Bute. Mure was M.P. for Renfrewshire from 1742 to 1761 and, as he excelled in the negotiation of parliamentary business and in constituency affairs, offered in 1757 to undertake the management of Lord Bute's neglected Scottish estates. In 1761 he was made a Baron of the Scottish Exchequer which removed him from parliament though not from a place of influence in Scotland. In the 1770s he appears to have been on terms of close friendship with the Adam brothers whom he advised financially at the time of the Adelphi lottery. His nephew Hutchinson Mure of Great Saxham (Pl. 13) was also an Adam client. Baron Mure died in 1776, aged 58, not long after Caldwell had been completed (Namier & Brooke, vol. II).

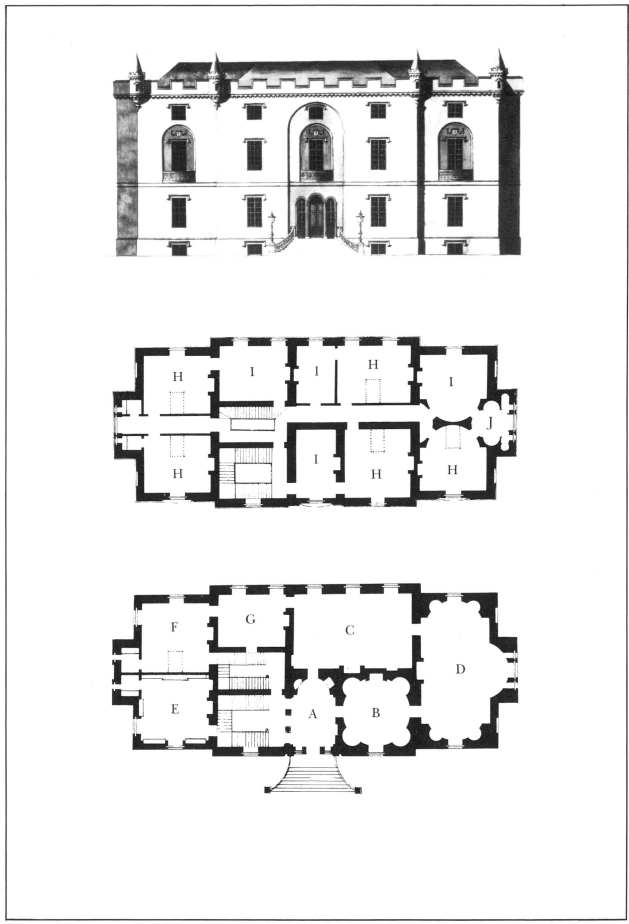

Pl. 36

Plate 37

Design in the castle style for Caldwell House, Beith, Ayrshire, for Baron Mure of Caldwell.

Rear elevation with the basement and second-floor plans of a rectangular house, with battlemented parapets and angle bartizans.

The drawings reproduced here are taken from a set of finished design drawings in the Scottish Record Office (RHP 2549). The use of the rooms, indicated in the office copy drawings (vol. 37, nos. 70–77), is as follows:

A	Kitchen	E	Servant's hall	I	Wine cellar
B	Scullery	F	Porter's room	J	Bedchamber
C	Butler	G	Men servants' bedroom	K	Servant's bedroom
D	Housekeeper	H	Women servants' bedroom		

The frontage extends 117 ft.
Original scale approximately 2 in. to 15 ft.: here 9 mm. to 10 ft.

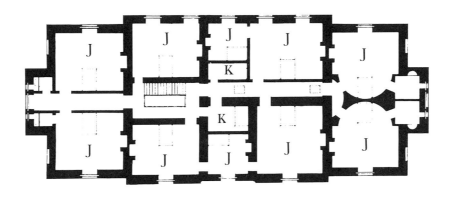

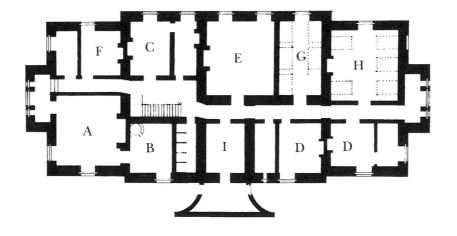

Pl. 37

Plate 38

Design for additions to Barnbougle Castle, Dalmeny, West Lothian, for Neil Primrose, Earl of Rosebery, K.T.

Principal elevation with the plan of the ground floor for extensive castle-style additions to a substantial L-shaped tower house.

Small-scale drawings for the first floor and rear elevation in vol. 46, nos. 132 and 133 (Pl. 39), establish this scheme as one for which drawings were prepared for publication. The plan reproduced here has been completed from the outline design drawing (vol. 37, no. 53) and the elevation is adapted from Adam's original presentation drawing in the possession of Lord Rosebery. In the original this is shown in a romantic landscape setting. The use of the rooms is as follows:

A	Porch	E	Coffee room	I	Lord Rosebery's dressing-room
B	Sub-hall	F	Billiards room	J	Valet
C	Servants' hall	G	Sub-parlour	K	Housekeeper
D	Kitchen and scullery	H	Gardrobe	L	Steward's room

The frontage extends 260 ft.
Scale here 7.5 mm. to 10 ft.

Robert Adam's proposed additions to Barnbougle Castle are dated 1774 and are linked by family tradition to Lord Rosebery's courtship of his second wife, Mary Vincent, only daughter of Sir Francis Vincent Bart. of Stoke D'Abernon in Surrey, whom he married on 17 July 1775. The Earl (1729–1814) was almost an exact contemporary of Robert Adam. As he was a younger son he had followed a business career in London until the death of his elder brother in August 1755 made him next in line to the title to which he succeeded in November the same year. He made the grand tour, meeting Casanova at Lausanne in 1760, and on his return to Britain assumed the traditional political role of his family as a representative government peer in the parliaments of 1768, 1774 and 1780. As a young man he struck Casanova as taciturn, timid and gauche (*Complete Peerage*, vol. XI, p. 135).

The drawings for this project preserved from the Adam office (vol. 37, nos. 51–58) tend to support the tradition that the commission was designed more for show than as the basis for a real building programme. No survey plans of the old buildings are known and the architects do not appear to have drawn up any plans for its upper floors or of their alterations to them. Four elevations (nos. 55–58) are experimental visual designs in which heavy and very soft pencil shadows have been added to rapidly sketched outlines as preparatory drawings for casting the shadows in the presentation set which Lord Rosebery no doubt showed to Mary Vincent. There is also an unusually evocative coloured elevational sketch of Barnbougle among the landscape compositions by Robert Adam in the print room of the National Galleries of Scotland.

These grandiose proposals were never taken further as the Primrose family lived in Dalmeny Castle until the Earl's death. About 1820 Barnbougle, which is dramatically situated on a promontory in the Firth of Forth, was blown up to become a picturesque ruin in the grounds of Dalmeny House, an early Tudoresque design by William Wilkins which the new Lord Rosebery had commissioned soon after he succeeded to the title. In 1881 the ruins of Barnbougle were restored to designs of Wardrop and Reid, though the low Victorian castle that survives today bears little resemblance to the massive old house recorded in Adam's designs (John Small, *Castles and Mansions of the Lothians* (1883), vol. 1).

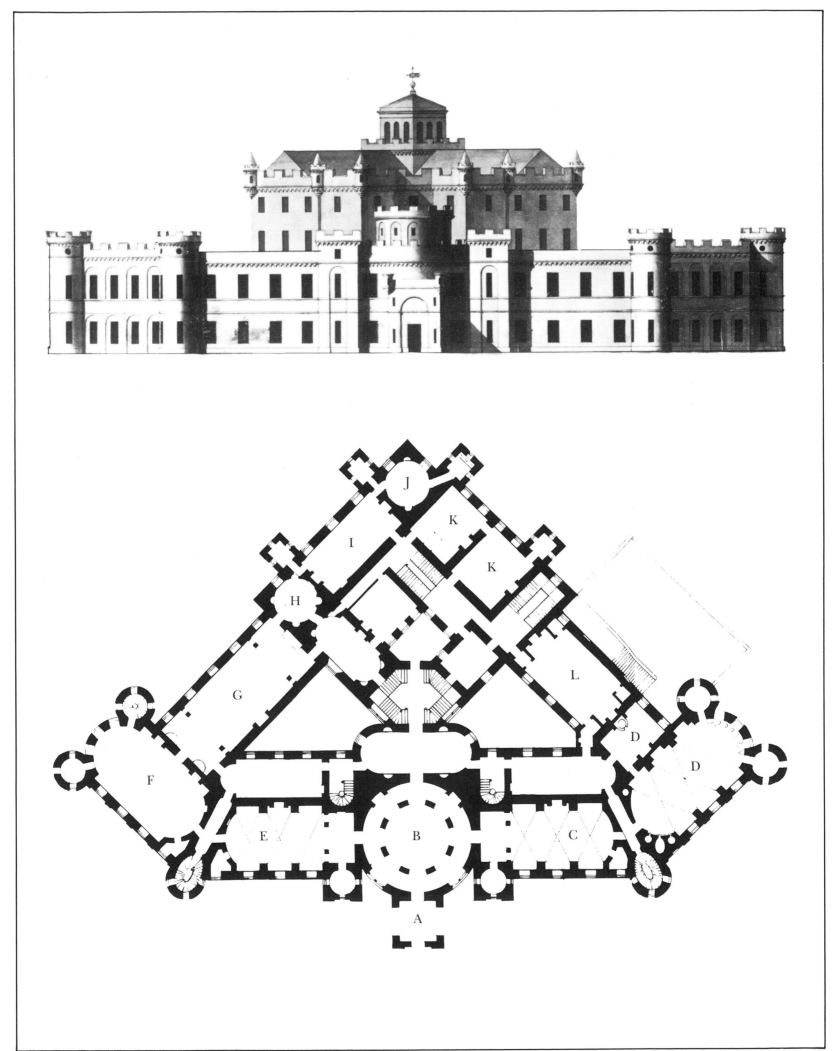

Pl. 38

Plate 39

Design for additions to Barnbougle Castle, Dalmeny, West Lothian, for Earl of Rosebery, K.T.

Rear elevation with the plan of the principal storey for extensive castle-style additions to a substantial L-shaped tower house.

Small-scale drawings. Originally two sheets. Vol. 46, nos. 132 and 133. *Insc. Earl of Roseberry.* The elevation in vol. 46 is only an outline with washes on the windows: that shown here is adapted from Adam's original presentation drawing in the possession of Lord Rosebery. In the original this is shown in a romantic landscape setting. The use of the rooms is as follows:

A	Tribune or 1st antechamber		G	Anteroom
B	Drawing-room or 2nd antechamber		H	Principal bedroom
C	Summer Eating-room or 3rd antechamber		I	Toilet room
D	Winter Eating-room or 3rd antechamber		J	Powder room
E	Library		K	Anteroom
F	Gallery for drawings etc.		L	Bedrooms

The frontage extends 260 ft.
Original scale 1 in. to 25 ft.: here 7.5 mm. to 10 ft.

As pure design the brothers' scheme for Barnbougle presents a paradox. On a number of occasions in the 1770s and 1780s Robert made designs for a type of castle based on a plan with two wings set at right angles to each other, or in the shape of a V, with the principal entrance in the re-entrant angle (see Pls. 44 and 48). There is a slight pencil plan and elevation (vol. 1, no. 38) which is possibly a proposal of this type for Barnbougle—wall thicknesses and certain dimensions seem to match the layout of the old castle—yet the design that was drawn up for presentation to Lord Rosebery and for publication rejects this layout even where the plan of the old building seemed to lend itself to such an arrangement. Here, rather than extend the building as two divergent wings, the Adams choose to close the main approach to the house with a straggling low block, 260 ft. long, which would have greatly reduced the effective height of the old tower. There is an uneasy dichotomy between the right-angled and square aesthetic used in the recasing of the old building and the curved bows and squat round towers proposed for the new ranges.

The inflated nature of this proposal recalls James Adam's schemes for Lowther Castle, Westmorland of 1767–71 (vol. 33, nos 35–54). A general vagueness may be noted in the uses proposed for different rooms—a summer and winter dining-room and many anterooms whose function is not defined—as if the architects had been asked to design grandly and to give their genius free rein. Few valets can have been accommodated in eighteenth-century Scotland in a rotunda which was to be 16 ft. in diameter with four matching niches and few earls in a bedroom 35 by 16 ft. with a double screen of columns and a dressing-room of identical dimensions on the floor below!

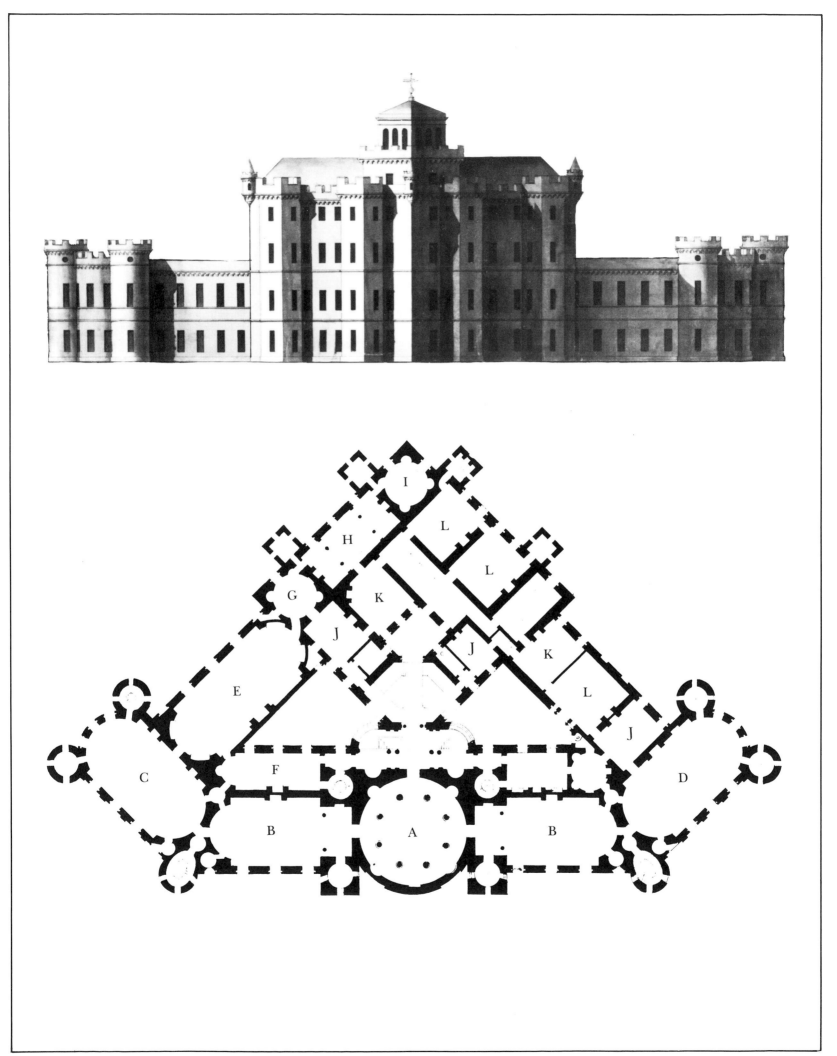

Pl. 39

Plate 40

Designs for a house in the castle style for Edward Smith-Stanley, Earl of Derby, at The Oaks, Sutton, Surrey: the first scheme.

Front elevation with the basement and the ground-floor plans of a large rectangular castle with a polygonal central tower and square corner turrets to the main block and complex polygonal and gabled pavilions linked by straight wings.

This design is recorded on six separate sheets. Vol. 29, nos. 25–30. *Insc. Castle of the Oaks, one of the seats of The Earl of Derby, South Front* and *Plan of the Principal Story of Oaks Castle* Etc. The use of the rooms is as follows:

A	Hall	G	Dressing-room	M	Steward
B	Stairs	H	Cabinet	N	Butler
C	Saloon	I	China closet	O	Housekeeper
D	Eating-room	J	Kitchen	P	Still room
E	Drawing-room	K	Scullery	Q	Cellars
F	Bedchamber	L	Servant's hall		

The frontage extends 192 ft.
Original scales: plan $1\frac{1}{4}$ in. to 10 ft.: elevation $\frac{3}{4}$ in. to 10 ft.: here 7.5 mm. to 10 ft.

As Lord Stanley, the Earl of Derby (1752–1834) had been one of the Adam brothers' most magnificent patrons, rebuilding his house in Grosvenor Square between 1773 and 1775 and employing the architects to design an elaborate and richly finished *fête* pavilion erected at The Oaks for a reception held there on his marriage in June 1774 to Lady Elizabeth Hamilton, daughter of the 6th Duke of Hamilton. Both these commissions are illustrated in *The Works*, vol. II and III and in Bolton 1922, chapters 19 and 20.

In 1776 Lord Stanley succeeded his grandfather as 12th Earl of Derby and soon after employed the Adams to prepare four sets of designs for a castle-style mansion at The Oaks, a small estate near Epsom which had belonged to his aunt, Lady Charlotte Stanley, and to her husband, General John Burgoyne. At the time of the *fête* The Oaks was still the property of the Burgoynes. It appears to have come to Lord Derby sometime after June 1776 when his aunt died and when General Burgoyne was fighting in America. The Burgoynes had added to The Oaks a large ballroom, richly decorated with neo-classical plasterwork and elliptical apses at either end. This work, which is attributed to Sir Robert Taylor (Marcus Binney, *Sir Robert Taylor* (London, 1984), p. 64), is the only part of the old house retained in the Adams' schemes, forming a separate pavilion on the right-hand side of the entrance front.

The Adams' designs for The Oaks are graded in a descending order of cost. This scheme, the largest, is noted in pencil on the main floor plan 'Design A £11,000'. None of the schemes illustrated here was built, though Lord Derby did embark on a comprehensive remodelling of the house about 1777, including much new work, for which a pencil sketch survives in vol. 1, no. 25. Within a year this rebuilding was to be set aside as a result of an intrigue between Lady Derby and the good-looking but unscrupulous Duke of Dorset, resulting in the break-up of Lord Derby's marriage. When the Earl succeeded to the title Robert Adam had prepared a fantastic scheme, exhibiting very fully the megalomania of the period, to convert the ancestral seat of Knowsley Park, Lancashire, into a gargantuan castle 472 ft. long (vol. 33, nos. 71 and 72). The discovery of Lady Derby's affair with the Duke put an end to all these schemes (*The Complete Peerage*, vol. IV, pp. 218–19; *D.N.B.* Burgoyne). The house that Adam began at The Oaks is illustrated in Rowan 1985(b).

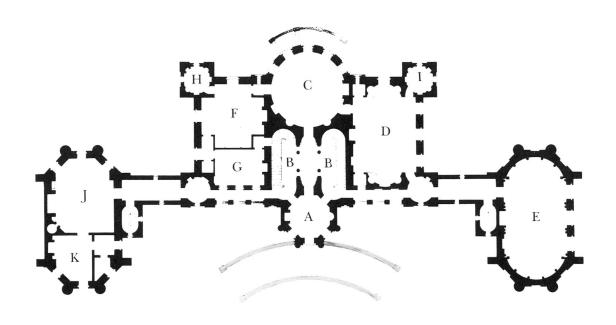

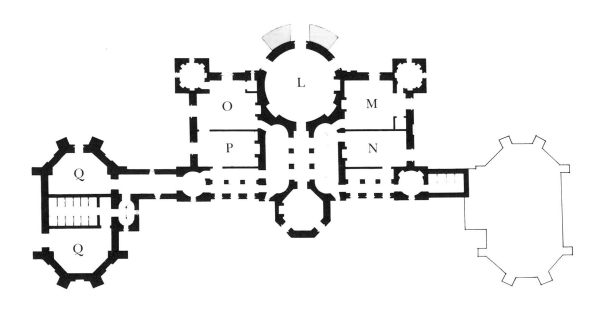

Pl. 40

Plate 41

Designs for a house in the castle style for the Earl of Derby, at The Oaks, Sutton, Surrey : the first scheme.

Rear elevation with the first-floor and attic plan of a large rectangular castle with an arcaded and battlemented circular tower in the centre of the garden front.

Originally three sheets. Vol. 29, nos. 26 and 29. *Insc. Castle of The Oaks, one of the Seats of The Earl of Derby, North Front* and *Plan of the one pair Story of Oaks Castle* Etc. The use of the rooms is as follows:

A   Bedchambers   B   Dressing closets

The frontage extends 192 ft.
Original scales: plan $1\frac{1}{4}$ in. to 10ft.: elevation $\frac{3}{4}$ in. to 10 ft.: here 7.5 mm. to 10 ft.

All four of the Adams' schemes for The Oaks date from 1777, the year in which Culzean Castle, which marks the introduction of a new and more decisive type of massing in their castles, was begun (Pl. 53). The design published here makes good use of the round corner turrets that were to become a leitmotif in the articulation of an Adam castle and also introduces, in the great drum tower on the garden front, a feature that was to reappear at Dalquharran, Pitfour, Culzean itself and in Robert's late proposals for Findlater Castle, Castle Semple (vol. 30, nos. 79 and 80) and Blair Drummond. Though Adam had been scornful of the plan of Penicuik House, Midlothian, built by John Baxter to designs of the proprietor Sir James Clerk in 1762 (*Country Life*, 15 and 22 Aug. 1968), it is noteworthy that the duplication of identical oval staircases which that design had introduced is a feature that occurs in several of Adam's own proposals in later years. In this volume duplicate staircases, which may also be derived from Vanbrugh's example, appear at High Down, in this design for Oaks Castle, and at Bewley, Findlater and Mauldslie Castles (Pls. 11, 48, 58 and 62).

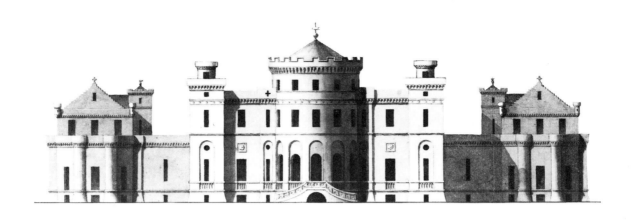

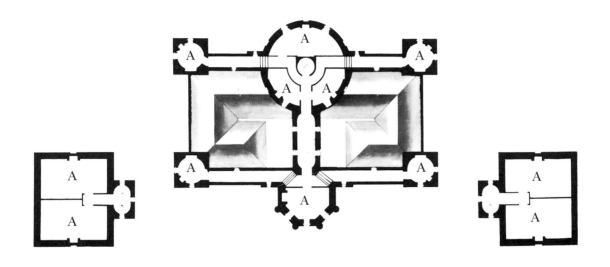

Pl. 41

Plate 42

Designs for a house in the castle style for the Earl of Derby, at The Oaks, Sutton, Surrey: the second scheme.

Front elevation with the basement and ground-floor plans of a square castle with a polygonal central tower on the entrance front and a round saloon at the rear. Complex polygonal and gabled pavilions are linked to the castle by straight wings.

This design is recorded on two sheets, each with two plans and an elevation (as reproduced here and in Pl. 43). Vol. 29, nos. 31 and 32. The layout of these drawings (and of those for the third and fourth scheme for Lord Derby's castle) has the appearance of a page that has been prepared with some sort of publication in view. This drawing is inscribed along the right-hand side at right angles to the plans *A second elevation & plans of Oaks Castle one of the Seats of the Earl of Derby*. The use of the rooms is as follows:

A	Hall	F	Kitchen	K	Beer cellar
B	Saloon	G	Steward's room	L	Wine cellar
C	Eating-room	H	Writing-room	M	Butler
D	Drawing-room	I	Housekeeper	N	Pantry
E	Lord Derby's bedroom	J	Servants' hall	O	Valet's room

The frontage extends 150 ft.
Original scale $\frac{3}{4}$ in. to 10 ft.: here 10 mm. to 10 ft.

This design which retains the complex pavilions of the largest scheme and reduces the house from an oblong to a square is noted in pencil on no. 31, 'Design B £8,903.12s'.

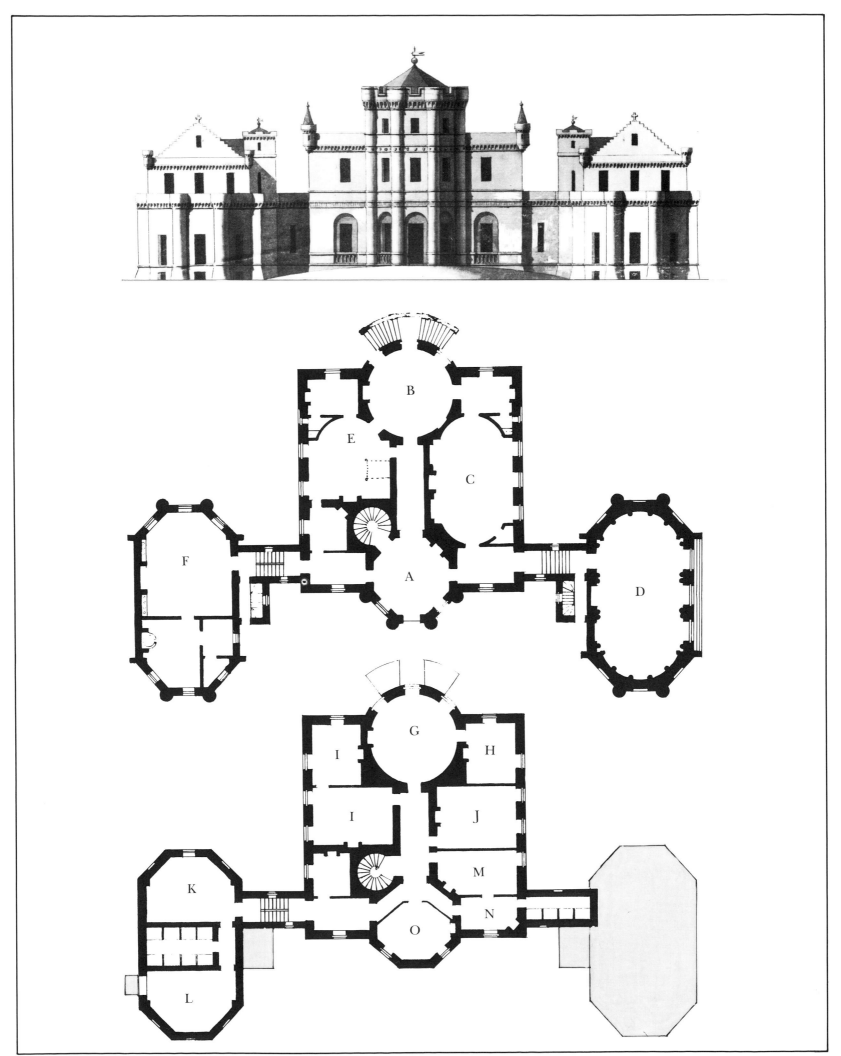

Pl. 42

Plate 43

Design for a house in the castle style for the Earl of Derby, at The Oaks, Sutton, Surrey: the second scheme.

Rear elevation with plans of the first-floor, attics and roofs of a square castle with polygonal pavilions.

Originally one sheet as reproduced here. Vol. 29, no. 32. *Insc.* (along one side) *A second elevation & plan of Oaks Castle one of the seats of the Earl of Derby, North Front, Plan of the towers and roofs* and *Plan of the one pair story*. The use of the rooms is as follows:

A	Bedchambers	C	Servants' bedrooms
B	Dressing-rooms		

The frontage extends 150 ft.
Original scale $\frac{3}{4}$ in. to 10 ft.: here 10 mm. to 10 ft.

Pl. 43

Plate 44

Design for a villa in the castle style for the Earl of Derby, at The Oaks, Sutton, Surrey : the third scheme.

Front elevation with the basement and ground-floor plans of a V-shaped castle linked by quadrant wings to astylar classical pavilions.

This design is recorded on two sheets, each with two plans and an elevation (as reproduced here and in Pl. 45). Vol. 29, nos. 33 and 34. *Insc.* (along one side) *A third Elevation & Plans of Oaks Castle one of the seats of the Earl of Derby, South front. Plan of the Principal story, Plan of the Basement story.* The use of the rooms is as follows:

A	Hall and stairs	F	Dressing-rooms	J	Housekeeper
B	Saloon	G	Kitchen	K	Butler
C	Eating-room	H	Steward's room	L	Valet's room
D	Drawing-room	I	Servants' hall	M	Footmen's hall
E	Lord Derby's bedroom				

The frontage extends 142 ft.
Original scale $\frac{3}{4}$ in. to 10 ft.: here 10 mm. to 10 ft.

This design, which dates from 1777, is remarkable as an early instance of Adam's experimentation with plans that are developed on unusual axes. The V-plan introduced here was to recur in proposals for a castle for John Robinson at Harwich in 1779 (vol. 37, nos. 81–86), where the access is reversed and the round tower, which houses the main sitting-room is placed at the apex of the V. The same basic scheme is used in the design for Bewley Castle (Pl. 48) and, in a modified form at Walkinshaw (Pl. 35).

The treatment of the pavilions in this scheme is curious, as Adam seems wilfully to reject the exact symmetry which could have been achieved by extending the kitchen block at the southwest corner to match the polygonal end of General Burgoyne's earlier ballroom. As the elevational treatment suggested for the pavilions is unlike the brothers' normal classical manner it may be that this drawing records the original appearance of Sir Robert Taylor's additions to the old property (see Pl. 40) and that Adam proposed the mixture of styles exhibited here as a consciously historicist picturesque element: a baronial castle to which classical pavilions had later been added. This scheme is noted in pencil 'Design C £5,589.14s'.

Pl. 44

Plate 45

Design for a villa in the castle style for the Earl of Derby, at The Oaks, Sutton, Surrey: the third scheme.

Rear elevation with the first-floor, attic and roof plans of a V-shaped castle linked by quadrant wings to astylar classical pavilions. A tall round tower occupies the re-entrant angle of the V.

Originally one sheet as reproduced here. Vol. 29, no. 33. *Insc.* (along one side) *A third Elevation & Plans of Oaks Castle one of the seats of the Earl of Derby, North Front, Plan of the one pair story* and *Plan of the Circular Tower and Roofs.* The use of the rooms is as follows:

A   Bedchambers   B   Dressing-rooms

The frontage extends 142 ft.
Original scale $\frac{3}{4}$ in. to 10 ft.: here 10 mm. to 10 ft.

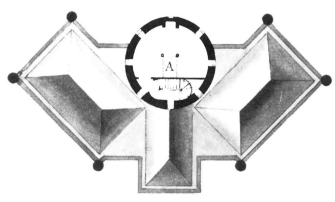

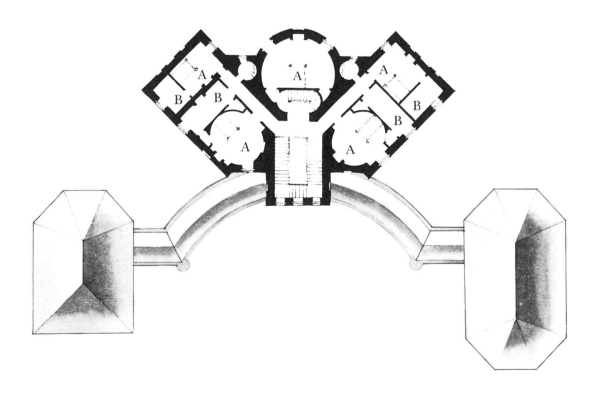

Pl. 45

Plate 46

Design for a villa in the castle style for the Earl of Derby, at The Oaks, Sutton, Surrey : the fourth scheme.

Front elevation with the basement and ground-floor plans of a small rectangular castle linked by straight wings to astylar classical pavilions.

This design is recorded on two sheets, each with two plans and an elevation (as reproduced here and in P. 47). Vol. 29, nos. 35 and 36. *Insc.* (along one side) *The 4 Elevation & Plans of Oaks Castle one of the seats of the Earl of Derby marked D. Plan of the Principal Story* and *Plan of the Ground Story*. The use of the rooms is as follows:

A	Hall	G	Kitchen
B	Saloon	H	Steward's room
C	Eating-room	I	Housekeeper
D	Drawing-room	J	Servants' hall
E	Lord Derby's bedroom	K	Butler
F	Dressing-rooms	L	Valet

The frontage extends 142 ft.
Original scale $\frac{3}{4}$ in. to 10 ft.: here 10 mm. to 10 ft.
Like the previous 'Design C' this, the smallest version of Adam's proposed new castle at The Oaks, seems to retain the exterior of Sir Robert Taylor's ballroom without alteration, balancing it on the west by a similar, though not identical block. The castle or main house is reduced to an architecture of great simplicity, reminiscent of Vanbrugh's small houses, where massing alone contributes a sense of presence to the design. Though a round saloon in the centre of the garden front was to become a common feature in later Georgian domestic architecture, this design of 1777 is the first occasion on which Adam expresses the saloon as a separate round tower. It may be noted also that the tower projects well beyond the line of the façade so that more than half its circumference is exposed. Adam was to use this precise position for his circular tower on the north front of Culzean in 1785 and a similar projection is envisaged in the villa based on the design of Lord Delaval's house at Cleremont (see Pl. 5). This small design, where the front of the house itself is reduced to 60 ft., was estimated to cost £5,404.5s. The plan of Dalquharran (Pl. 51) begun by Adam in 1784 clearly derives from this scheme.

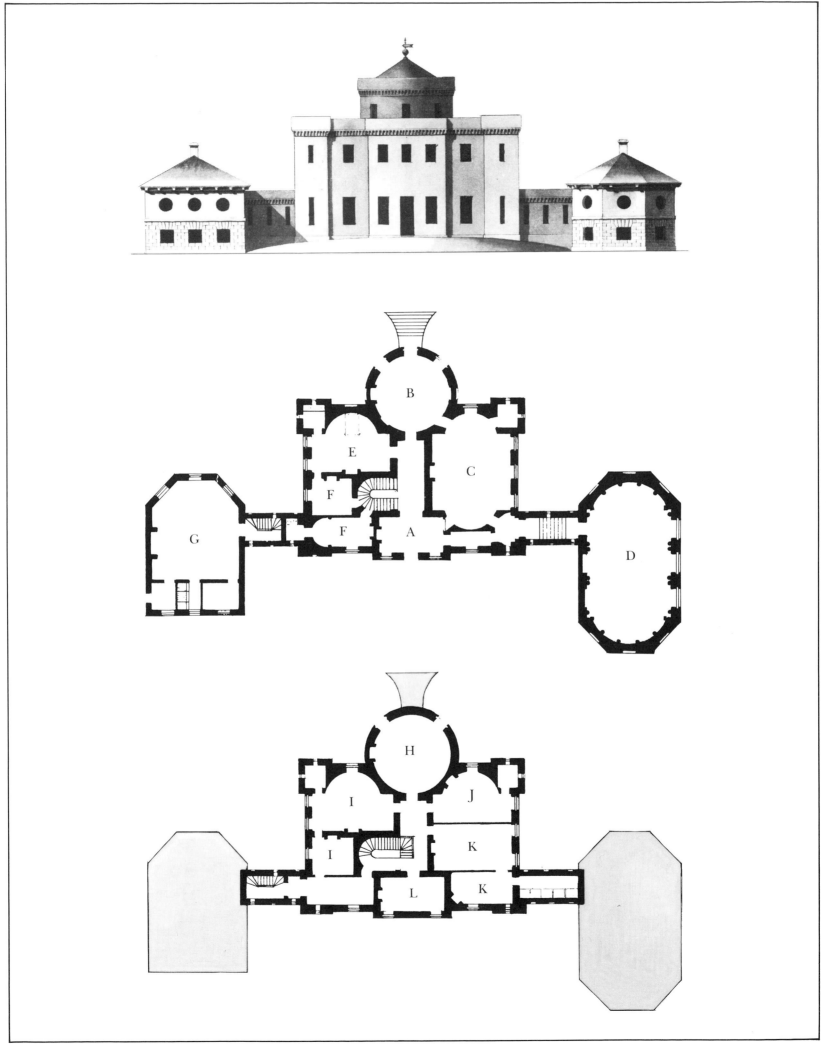

Pl. 46

Plate 47

Design for a villa in the castle style for the Earl of Derby, at The Oaks, Sutton, Surrey : the fourth scheme.

Rear elevation with the first floor, attic and roof plans of a small rectangular castle with a round tower in the centre and linked by straight wings to astylar classical pavilions.

Originally one sheet as reproduced here. Vol. 29, no. 35. *Insc.* (along one side) *The 4th Elevation & Plans of Oaks Castle one of the seats of the Earl of Derby, Plan of the one pair story* and *Plan of the tower and roofs*. The use of the rooms is as follows:

A   Bedrooms   B   Closets

The frontage extends 142 ft.
Original scale $\frac{3}{4}$ in. to 10 ft. : here 10 mm. to 10 ft.

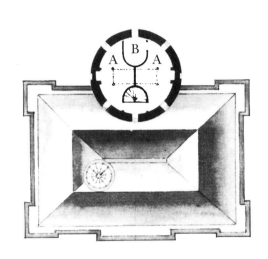

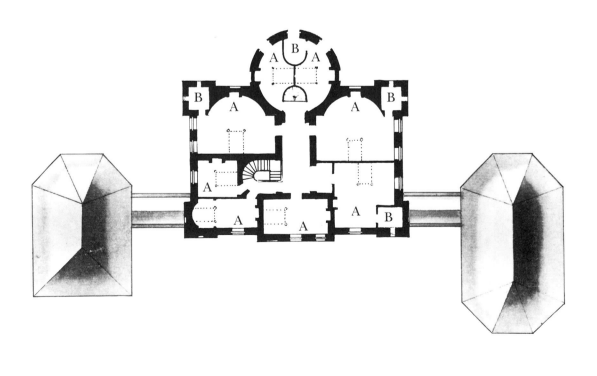

Pl. 47

Plate 48

Design for a house in the castle style at Bewley, Kiltarlity, Beauly, Inverness-shire for Simon Fraser, Master of Lovat, M.P.

Ground-floor plan and front elevation of a castle and its surrounding outworks, laid out in the shape of a V with a circular saloon at the apex and the entrance in the re-entrant angle.

None of the drawings in vol. 46 prepared for publication records this scheme. However the plan, reproduced here, from vol. 30, no. 74, is drawn to the 'miniature' scale associated with the schemes which the brothers intended to publish and may have been prepared with this in view. In the original, the walls of the outworks are drawn in outline. *Insc. Plan of the Principal Story of a new Design for Bewley Castle Adelphi 21 Oct 1777.* The elevation is a modern drawing. The use of the rooms is indicated as follows:

A	Hall	D	Eating-room
B	Saloon	E	Bedchambers
C	Drawing-room	F	Dressing-rooms

The outworks measure 275 by 253 ft.
Original scale 1 in. to 25 ft.: here 7.5 mm. to 10 ft.

General Simon Fraser (1726–82), the eldest son and heir of Lord Lovat, who with his father took part in the 1745 Jacobite rising, surrendered on 13 August 1746 and was granted a free pardon in May 1750. During the Seven Years' War he raised a regiment of Highlanders, the 78th or Fraser Highlanders, drawn largely from his own clansmen, with whom he served in North America under General Wolfe and in Portugal. From 1761 until his death he represented Inverness in the House of Commons and in 1774, in consideration of his military services, obtained by Act of Parliament the restoration of all the family estates, forfeited by his father, subject to the payment of £20,983 (*The Complete Peerage,* VIII, pp. 195–96).

The first house to be built on the estate was 'a very plain but commodious building' erected soon after 1755 to house the government factor during the forfeiture (*Reports on the Annexed Estates 1755–1769,* H.M.S.O.; 1973]. Adam's scheme was intended to replace this utilitarian structure. Nothing seems to have been carried out by General Fraser or by his half-brother Archibald, who succeeded in 1782. In 1838 the sixteenth Lord Lovat commissioned William Burn to make castellated additions to the factor's house, which survived until 1886 when a new castle was built to designs of James Maitland Wardrop. In the nineteenth century the name of the house was changed to Beaufort Castle.

In addition to the drawings reproduced here, two sketch plans of Bewley are in vol. 2, nos. 204 and 225, which provide for slightly different accommodation. Two perspective drawings showing the castle in a bleak moorland setting, like some forlorn military outpost, are in vol. 30, nos. 77 and 78. These are both dated 'Adelphi, 21 October 1777'.

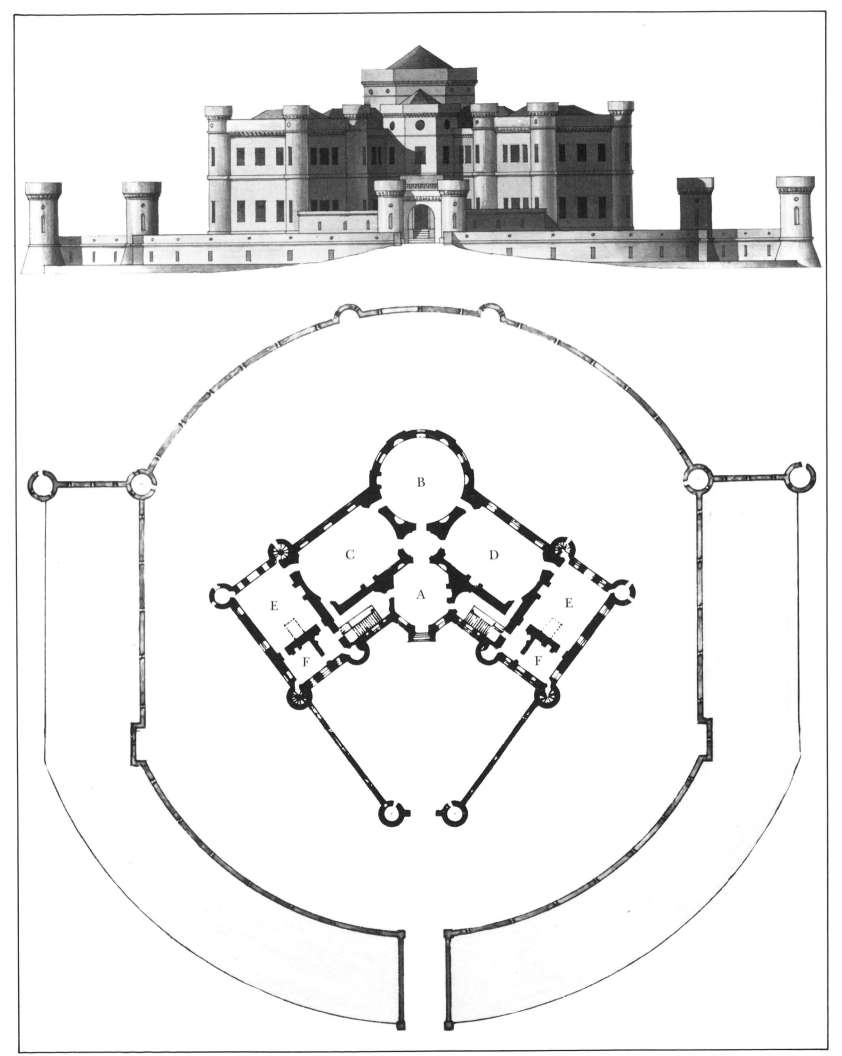

A

B

C

D

E

E

F

F

Pl. 48

Plate 49

Design for a house in the castle style at Bewley, Kiltarlity, Beauly, Inverness-shire, for Simon Fraser, Master of Lovat, M.P.

Principal and rear elevations with the first-floor plan of a castle laid out in the shape of a V with round turrets at the corners of each block, a polygonal entrance tower and a taller circular tower at the meeting of the two rear elevations.

The plan is a small-scale drawing. Vol. 30, no. 75. In the original it is drawn only in outline. The elevations, vol. 30, nos. 72 and 73, are drawn to a large scale. *Insc. One pair story of Bewley Castle. Bewley Castle* and *Another view of Bewley Castle.* A plan of the basement story, not reproduced here, is in vol. 30, no. 76 and the attic and roofs are in vol. 1, no. 138. The use of the rooms is as follows:

A	Anteroom	C	Dressing-rooms
B	Bedchambers		

The frontage extends 148 ft.
Original scales: plan 1 in. to 25 ft.: elevations 1 in. to 10 ft.: here 10 mm. to 10 ft.

Pl. 49

Plate 50

Design for a house in the castle style for Mr. Stevenson.

Principal elevation with the basement and ground-floor plans of a long rectangular castle with a round tower on the entrance front and a bowed projection set between circular turrets at the back. Courtyards of stables and farm offices extend the length of the façade.

Small-scale drawings. Originally on two sheets. Vol. 46, nos. 141 and 142. *Insc. Unknown.* The use of the rooms indicated on the design drawings, vol. 37, nos. 117–119, is as follows:

A	Hall	G	Scullery
B	Dining-room	H	Housekeeper
C	Drawing-room	I	Dairy
D	China closet	J	Brewhouse
E	Study	K	Cow byre
F	Kitchen	L	Stables

The frontage extends 200 ft.
Original scale 1 in. to 25 ft.: here 10 mm. to 10 ft.

The design drawings for this scheme are dated 'Adelphi, 10 July 1783'. Among the Adam castles the house, which was never built, is unusual for the length of its façade and for the steeply pitched almost 'French' roofs over the outer bays at either end of the front. The treatment of the central round tower, with its shallow arcading, was to reappear in 1785 in the elevation of the kitchen block at Culzean Castle, while the shallow bow held between turrets on the garden front may be seen as a development of the bow on the garden front at Oxenfoord Castle of 1780 and as a precursor of similar features at Airthrey and Mauldslie Castles (Pls. 61 and 63). Sketches for this design are in vol. 10, nos. 76 and 77.

   The identification of this scheme with a Mr. Stevenson is one of the clearest cases where an inscription on an Adam office drawing has been amplified by additions at a later date. Thus vol. 37, no. 117, was originally titled 'Plan of the sunk story' to which has been added 'of a Castle for Mr. Stevenson'. Not all the names added in this way prove to be correct and it may be that Mr. Stevenson's castle was really designed for a different client (see Introduction, n. 17). If the extra annotation is correct the design may have been prepared for Nathaniel Stevenson of Braidwood near Carluke, Lanarkshire. A later castle-style design for Mr. Stevenson by James Adam (Pl. 64) is annotated 'Elevation towards the river' and the Braidwood estate is described in 1839 as 'occupying a commanding situation and high ground which overhangs the vale of Clyde' (George Vere Irving and A. Murray, *The Upper Ward of Lanarkshire, Described and Delineated* (Glasgow, 1864), p. 441). The house proposed here, with its close association with farmyards and stables, and its simple arrangement of public rooms is evidently a design for a landed family of modest consequence. An alternative identity for Mr. Stevenson could perhaps be Dr. Alexander Stevenson, a physician in Glasgow noted in the political report on voters prepared by William Adam in 1788 as 'pretty independent' with a family 'and nephews to provide for' (*Report*, pp. 34 and 145). The brothers also designed a ceiling (vol. 30, no. 140) for a Mrs. Stevenson living at Hertford Street, London; her identity is not known. (*Burke's Landed Gentry* (1894), Stevenson of Braidwood).

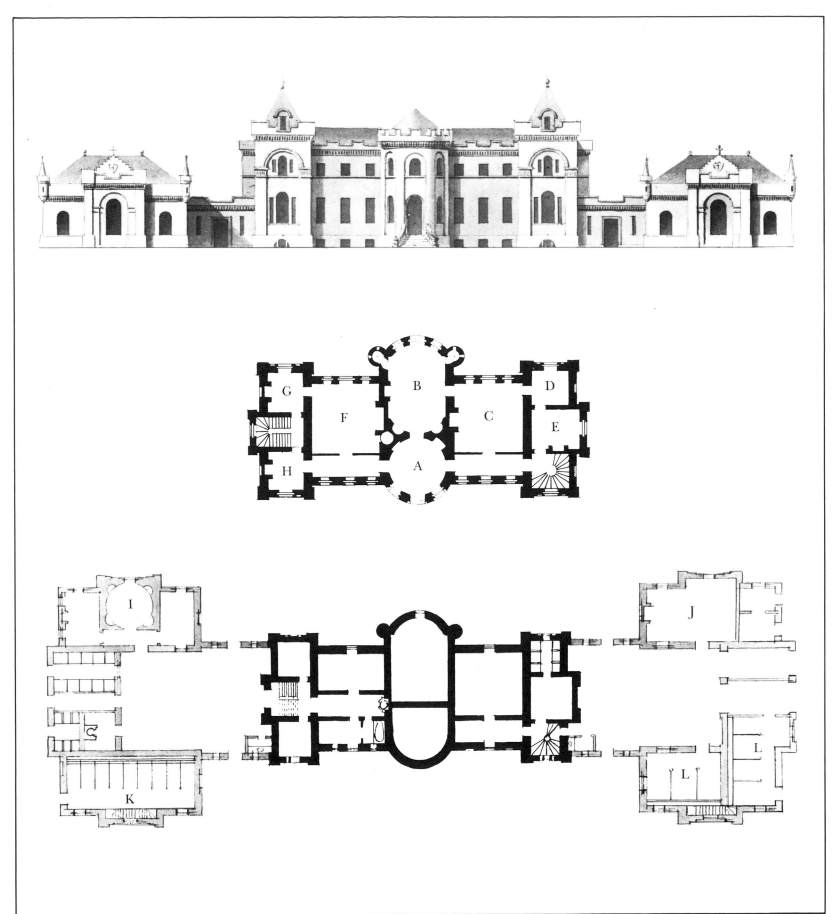

Pl. 50

Plate 51

Design for Dalquharran Castle, Dailly, Ayrshire,
for Thomas Kennedy of Dunure Esquire.

Ground-floor plan of a large rectangular castle with its forecourt, lodges, stables and coach houses; also the elevation of the stable block fronting the house.

One sheet of small-scale drawings. Vol. 46, no. 147 (reproduced on Pl. 52), records this design as one which was intended for publication. A second of the same dimensions, showing presumably the ground-floor plan and front elevation, has been torn from the same page, f. 76. The plan reproduced here is taken from the office outline plan vol. 31, no. 47 inked in for this publication. The elevation is a modern drawing based on vol. 31, no. 50. The use of the rooms is as follows:

A	Hall	F	Stables
B	Eating-room	G	Cow house
C	Drawing-room	H	Coach house
D	Bedchamber	I	Dairy
E	Dressing-room	J	Porter's lodge

The frontage, including the forecourt, extends 268 ft.
Scale 7.5 mm. to 10 ft.

Adam's client at Dalquharran, Thomas Kennedy of Dunure (c. 1740–1819), was married to the architect's niece, Jean, a daughter of John Adam of Blair Adam. Though relations between Robert and John became strained, the Kennedys of Dunure remained firm patrons of the younger brothers; their commission for the new house at Dalquharran offered Robert Adam a valuable opportunity to design a largish country house in his recently established castle style. In autumn 1781 Adam was asked both to consider a scheme to rehabilitate the sixteenth-century castle beside the Girvan Water and to draw up proposals for a new house. The schemes for the old castle (vol. 31, no. 41) are in an idiom similar to that developed for Caldwell and for the older parts of Barnbougle; the proposals for the new house are essentially similar to the design shown here (vol. 31, no. 39). Both date from February 1782.

The Kennedys chose the new house and between February and 10 May 1782 the scheme was developed in more detail. Plans that record this stage are a set of small drawings (vol. 1, nos. 195 and 197) and one plan (vol. 31, no. 44). These show a larger house than was built, with a more massive circular tower on the garden front lit by five (not three) windows, a crow-stepped gable between the turrets of the entrance front, of a type that reappears at Seton and Mauldslie Castles, and pointed pyramid roofs on the outer turrets. Nothing was done until the spring of 1785 when the plan of the house was fixed as it is shown here (vol. 31, no. 43). The full courtyard plan is dated 'Adelphi, 20 Nov. 1785' and is recorded in a diminutive perspective sketch (vol. 1, no. 262).

In execution the offices at Dalquharran were reduced to a single range fronting the principal façade of the house and linked to it by plain walls with simple gate piers. The drawing for this reduced scheme (vol. 31, no. 49) is dated '2 Jany 1789'. In that year Thomas Kennedy asked Adam for a note of the moneys he had paid his draughtsmen for working on plans for the house 'from 1781 to the month of August 1789'. It came to a total of £91.7s.1d. Kennedy paid his uncle-in-law £100 and in return Adam sent a design for the bookcases and plasterwork in the library at the top of the round tower (vol. 31, nos. 45 and 46), which dates from 23 April 1790. The building work at Dalquharran was superintended by Hugh Cairncross and the plasterwork was executed by James Nisbet. In 1881 the house was enlarged by F. T. R. Kennedy who added two plain wings which doubled the length of the façades. The building is now a ruin.

(Copies of two letters from Robert Adam to Thomas Kennedy in 1789 are in N.M.R.S.; see also A. H. Millar, *Castles and Mansions of Ayrshire* (Edinburgh, 1884); Rowan 1974c, p. 494; and *Burke's Landed Gentry* (1894), Kennedy of Dunure).

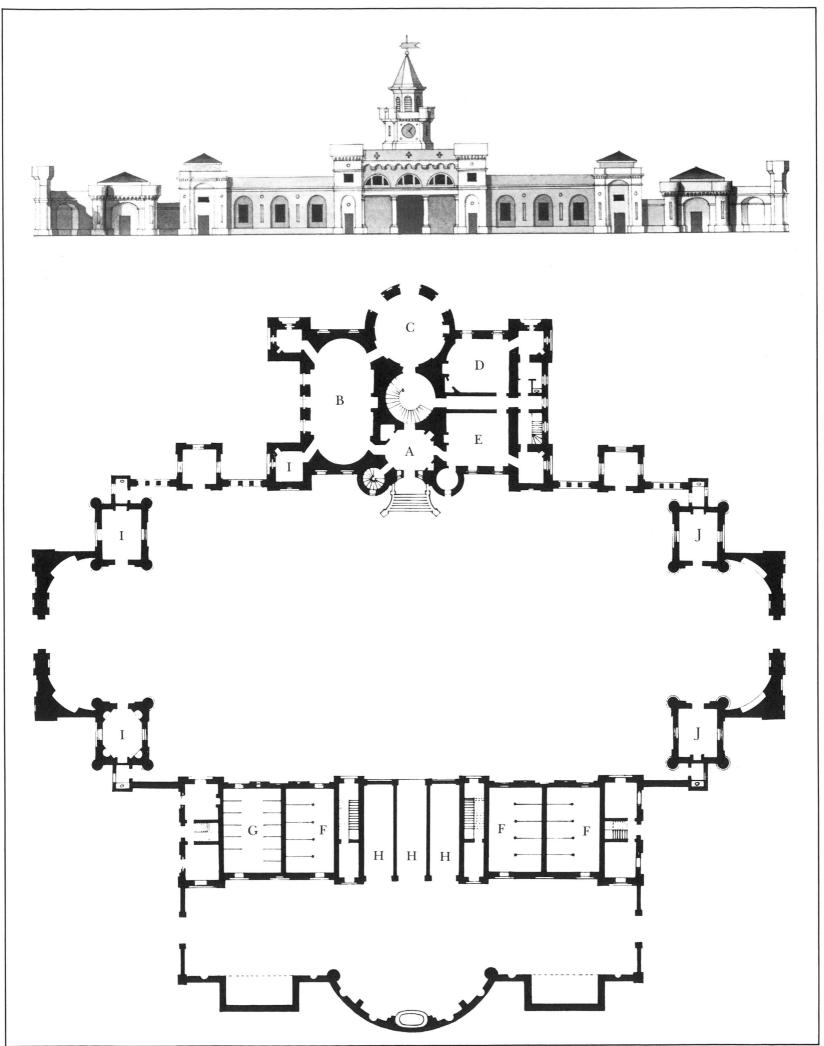

Pl. 51

Plate 52

Design for Dalquharran Castle, Dailly, Ayrshire,
for Thomas Kennedy of Dunure Esquire.

Front and rear elevations with the first-floor plan of a large rectangular castle with square corner turrets, a circular central staircase and a round tower in the centre of the garden front.

Small-scale drawing. Originally one sheet showing the plan and rear elevation. Vol. 46, no. 147. *Insc. Mr. Kennedy of Delquharran* [sic]. The entrance elevation reproduced here is a modern drawing based on the office outline copy of half the front in vol. 31, no. 50. The use of the rooms is not recorded.

The frontage extends 95 ft.
Original scale 1 in. to 25 ft.: here 10 mm. to 10 ft.

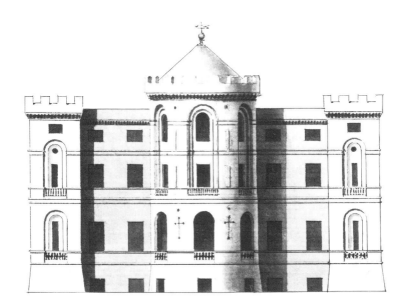

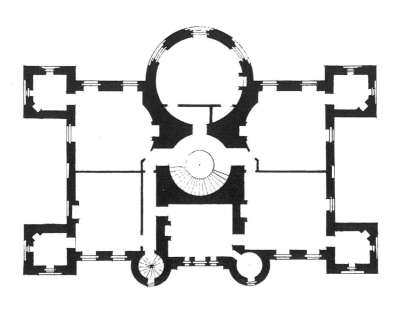

Pl. 52

Plate 53

Designs for Culzean Castle, Maybole, Ayrshire for David Kennedy, Earl of Cassillis.

Plan of the ground floor of a symmetrical rectangular castle showing the addition of a new range with a central round tower and irregularly grouped offices: also a pictorial elevation of the new work.

Two sheets of small-scale drawings, vol. 46, nos. 143 and 144 (reproduced as Pl. 54) record this scheme as one which was intended for publication. The elevation and plan shown here are reproduced from vol. 37, nos. 1 and 8. *Insc. North Front of Cullean* [sic] *Castle towards the sea with the new additions proposed for the Right Hon. the Earl of Cassillis.* The use of the rooms is as follows:

A	Hall	F	Kitchen	K	Cold Bath
B	Eating-room	G	Scullery	L	Dressing-rooms
C	Library	H	Housekeeper	M	Bake house
D	Buffet	I	Servants' hall	N	Brew house
E	Butler's pantry	J	Second Table-room		

The frontage extends 202 ft.
Original scale of elevation 1 in. to 10 ft.: here 10 mm. to 10 ft.

Culzean Castle was to become the largest single complex built in Adam castle style and is the subject of a separate article in Bolton 1922, vol. II, chapter 35. Comparatively few designs for the architecture of the house are preserved in the volumes in the Soane Museum (vol. 37, nos. 1–9), though there are many drawings for the ceilings, friezes, chimney-pieces and furniture. There is also a series of sketch views and preparatory designs (vol. 1, nos. 31–33, 35 and vol. 21, nos. 5–8) and an extensive though incomplete set of drawings from the house, now the property of the National Trust for Scotland.

As Culzean is a design that evolved over a period of more than twelve years, the progress of Adam's castle style may be charted in the growing boldness of its façades. The brothers had first been employed at Culzean by Sir Thomas Kennedy who, in a protracted lawsuit (where the judgement in his favour was given by another Adam client, Lord Mansfield), established his right to the earldom of Cassillis. For Sir Thomas the brothers made designs for a house to be built in the shape of an octagonal belvedere, but no work had been undertaken by 30 November 1775 when Kennedy, now Lord Cassillis, died. His younger brother David Kennedy, who succeeded as 10th Earl, was a member of the Faculty of Advocates in Edinburgh and had been M.P. for Ayrshire in the same parliament (1768–74) in which Robert Adam represented Kinross. The elder brother had perhaps already contemplated an extension of the old tower house at Culzean for it is stated in *The Scots Peerage* that the 10th Earl 'carried on the work of his brother and completed the building of the modern house of Culzean and the gardens' (vol. II, p. 492). However, no drawings survive for the house dated earlier than 1777 and it is clear that the castle as it developed is entirely due to commissions from the 10th Earl.

The plan shown here represents two distinct stages in the building's construction: the symmetrical suite of rooms arranged around a square (where the walls are shown in black) marks the limit of the first work of extension to the castle begun in 1777. Here the stairs and eating-room before it occupy the space of the old house to which the Adams made additions. The kitchen wing to the right and brew house and bath to the left were built early in the 1780s and were at first linked to the main house by haphazard older offices and yards which had existed at the back of the old castle. In 1785 the new north elevation of the house with the great round tower set above the cliffs was designed to replace these utilitarian buildings.

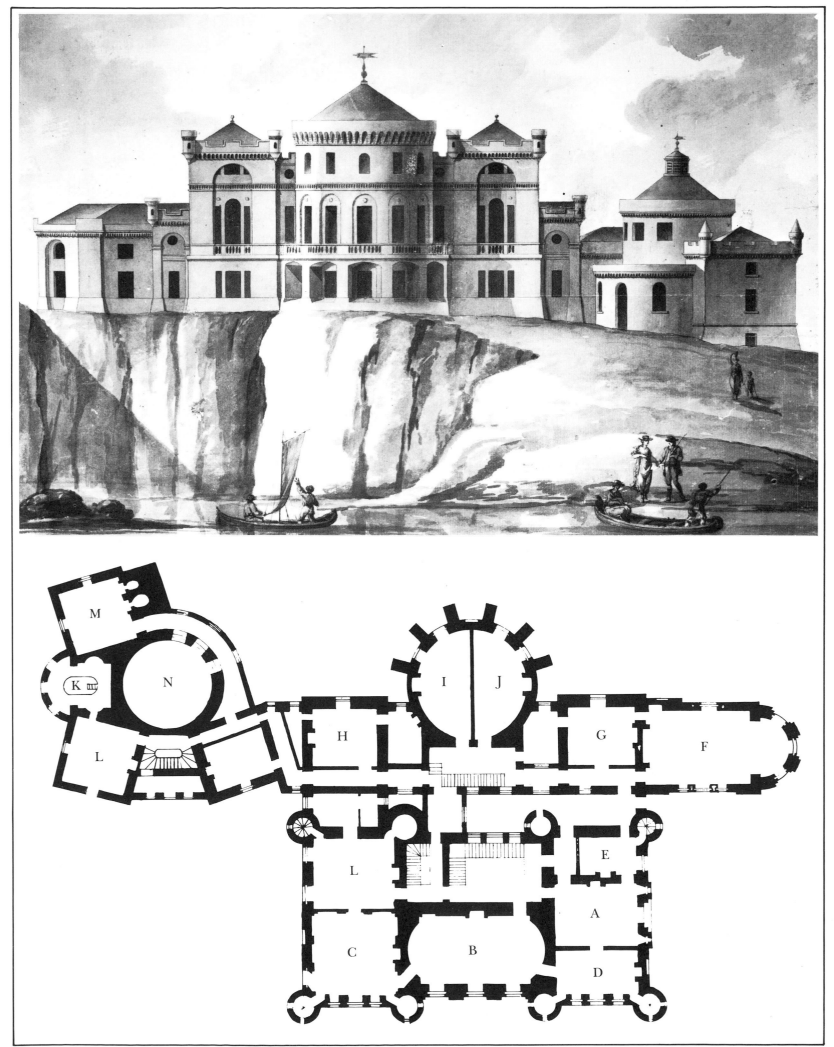

Pl. 53

Plate 54

Designs for Culzean Castle, Maybole, Ayrshire, for the Earl of Cassillis.

Plans of the ground floor and principal floor of the main block of the castle.

Small-scale drawings. Originally two sheets. Vol. 46, nos. 143 and 144. *Insc. Unknown.* The use of the rooms, as indicated on the design drawings, vol. 37, nos. 5 and 6, is as follows:

A	Drawing-rooms	G	Eating-room
B	Saloon	H	Buffet
C	Libraries	I	Hall
D	Bed chambers	J	Housekeeper
E	Dressing-rooms	K	Scullery
F	Ante-room		

Original scale 1 in. to 25 ft.: here 10 mm. to 10 ft.

These plans for the main block of Culzean record the house that developed from 1777 to 1791 when the great saloon on the north front was decorated. Comparison with the plan on the preceding page will show how the three stairs in the space between the eating-room to the south and the saloon on the north were removed to accommodate a new principal staircase designed on an oval plan in May 1787. This alteration necessitated some adjustment in the servant offices to the north, where a second service stair was inserted to the west of the lobby before the great saloon.

The new stair at Culzean, created as phase three in Lord Cassillis's building programme, must have given particular satisfaction to its architect as the germ of this idea had been in Adam's mind for sometime. The position of the stairs in the centre of the house may be traced back to some ideal projects by the Earl of Mar and to schemes by William Adam, senior, for houses at Tullibardin and Cumbernauld (*Vitruvius Scoticus*, Pls. 102 and 126). These designs provide a basis for the central stairs in many of the plans for houses published here (Pls. 5, 18, 19, 22, 29, 51 and 64). The version employed at Culzean gains grandeur from Adam's decision to limit the flights of steps to those that lead from the ground to the first floor; from his choice of an Imperial or double-return stair layout and from the continuous colonnade which surrounds the stair-well at first-and second-floor level. Prototypes for leaving the central space open may be found in a scheme for a classical *maison de plaisance* prepared for Culzean by J. Aulagnier of Marseilles in 1765 and, more particularly in Adam's own work, in the staircase at Home House, London, designed in 1773. The colonnade surround to the stair is anticipated in a design for York House, Pall Mall, by Sir William Chambers of 1760, exhibited in the following year, and in the principal stair at Wardour Castle, Wiltshire, designed by James Paine in 1770. In both these designs however the columns are restricted to a single floor. The Adam proposals for Great Saxham Hall, Wyke Manor and Findlater Castle (Pls. 13, 16, 58 and 59) all envisage stairs of the Culzean type. A section of this stair is given on Pl. 55.

These plans also provide a record of the new library with the altered kitchen arrangements below, which Adam intended to create in the northeast corner of the house. This last alteration was not carried out and the library remained on the lower floor at the southwest corner, the first part of the house to be built in 1777. In the later nineteenth century, when a new west wing was added to designs of Reid and Wardrop, the library and the eating-room changed places. At that time the dressing-room to the north of the library was absorbed to make one large room decorated in a competent neo-Adam style.

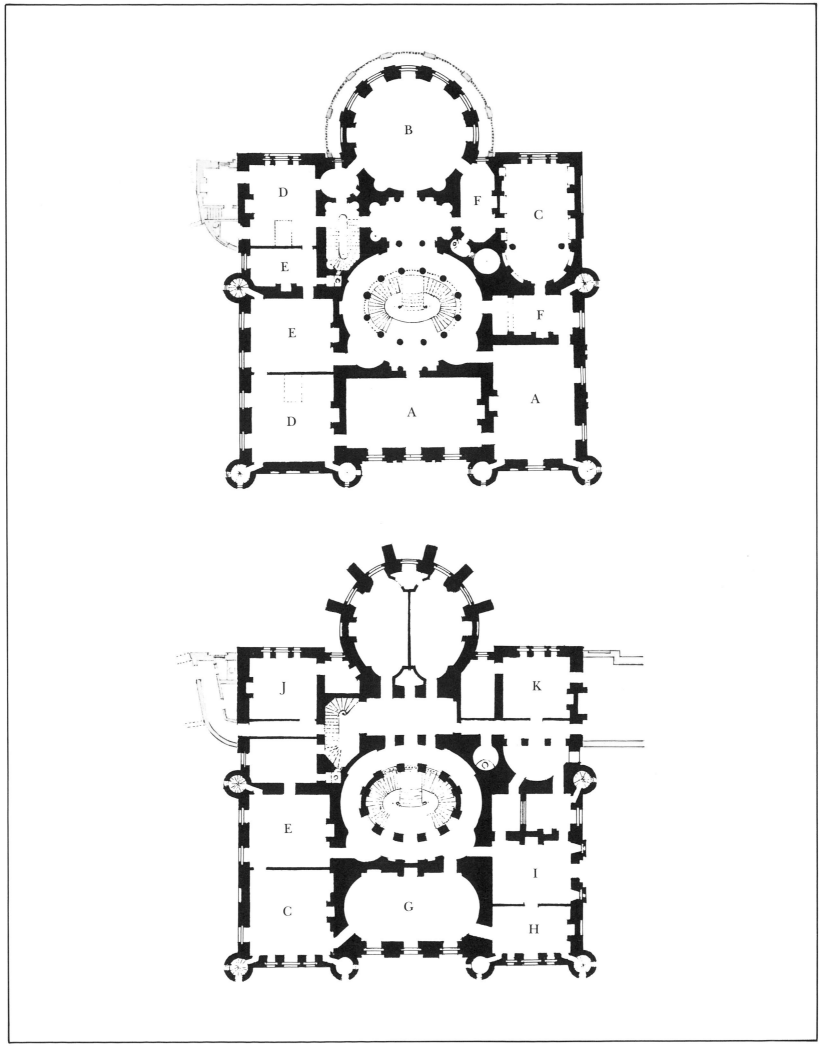

Pl. 54

Plate 55

Designs for Culzean Castle, Maybole, Ayrshire, for the Earl of Cassillis.

Elevation of the principal and entrance fronts with a longitudinal section through the main staircase and dressing-rooms.

Small-scale drawing. South front R.I.B.A. Drawings Collection, 86 × 125 mm. The side elevation is from vol. 37, no. 2 and the section, which in the original lacks any washes, is no. 4.

The frontages extend 100 and 114 ft.
Original scales 1 in. to 25 ft. and 1 in. to 10 ft.: here 10 mm. to 10 ft.

The small drawing of the south or principal front of Culzean, though more crudely finished than the 'miniature' designs in vol. 46, is executed to exactly the same scale and is unique, among the Adam drawings preserved outside the main collection in the Soane Museum, as the sole example of the type of drawing which was prepared for an engraver to copy. It may be one of the thirteen sheets which were removed from vol. 46 (see Introduction, p. 14) or it may have migrated earlier from the Adam office. The provenance of the drawing from the collection of Blackadder House, Berwickshire, suggests that it was drawn up in Edinburgh (*Catalogue of the Drawings Collection of the Royal Institute of British Architects*, vol. A, (London, 1968), p. 16).

The development of the Adam castle style which was to increase in bulk and in boldness in the 1780s is conveniently illustrated by a comparison of the architecture of the principal front of 1777 with the additions made to the north of the entrance from 1785. It will be noted that the new work is conceived on a larger scale and that walls are treated in a sculpturesque way. The detailing is bolder with tall relieving arches drafted across the façades, while the battlements are made up of increasingly bulky elements, culminating in the solid and heavily machicolated wall-head of the round tower, sited at the edge of a cliff.

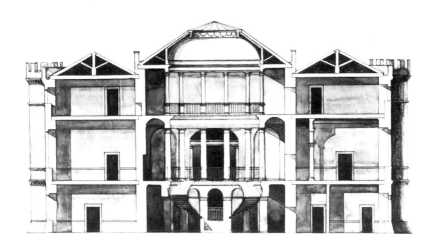

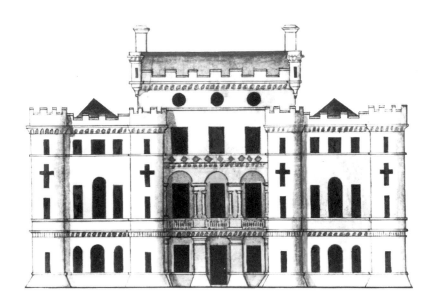

Pl. 55

Plate 56

Design for Seton Castle, Tranent, East Lothian, for Alexander Mackenzie of Portmore.

Front and rear elevations with the ground-floor plan of a large villa in the castle style with an enclosed forecourt and flanking U-shaped blocks of kitchen and stable offices.

Two sheets of small-scale drawings, vol. 46, no. 146, reproduced here, and no. 147 (Pl. 57), record this design as one which was intended for publication. *Insc. Principal front of Seton Castle.* The plan is taken from vol. 33, no. 94 and the front elevation is a modern drawing based on an office outline copy in vol. 33, no. 92. The use of the rooms is as follows:

A	Hall	G	Kitchen	L	Stables
B	Drawing-room	H	Sculleries	M	Cow house
C	Dining-room	I	Butler	N	Hen house
D	Bedroom	J	Dairy	O	Slaughter house
E	Dressing-rooms	K	Laundry	P	Coach houses
F	Business room				

The frontage extends 188 ft.
Original scale 1 in. to 25 ft.: here 10 mm. to 10 ft.

The site for Seton Castle was immediately beside the remains of old Seton Palace, a vast courtyard house, formerly the seat of the Earls of Wintoun whose estates were forfeited to the Crown after the 1715 rebellion. The palace was ruinous by 1789, when the British antiquary Francis Grose drew its remains and was soon to be used as a convenient quarry for the new house. The commission for Seton Castle dates from the summer of 1789, when Adam was in Scotland for his annual visit. The design proceeded quickly and was already carried to the stage of working drawings by December the same year. One alternative, suggested in the course of the design, was to propose a slightly deeper courtyard with two square turrets breaking forward from the sides of the kitchens and stable wings. This is recorded in a plan in vol. 33, no. 94, on which flaps of paper, to show the existing wings, have been overlaid.

The building contract for Seton (Scottish Record Office, G.D. 18, no. 4965) is dated 12 November 1789. By 26 April 1790 Paterson was writing from Edinburgh to report that the ruins had been cleared, that he and Mr. McKenzie had been to the site, where he had pointed out the extent of the house and where the great tower should stand, and that he had laid the foundation stone. By 3 May plans of the joisting were required and the house was roofed over before the end of the season. The interior was completed in the spring and early summer of 1791. Paterson had asked Adam to send moulds from London for the plasterwork decoration, which arrived in April that year, and the final furnishing of the castle will have been overseen by Adam himself who reached Edinburgh on his last northern visit on 22 May and who dined with his client at Seton on 11 June (*Paterson Correspondence*; Fleming 1968a; J. P. Lawson, *Scotland Delineated* (1847), vol. I, p. 185).

Alexander Mackenzie (1767–96), a lieutenant-colonel in the 21st Dragoons, was the eldest son of Alexander Mackenzie of Portmore, Peebleshire. Like Robert Haldane of Airthrey Mackenzie was one of the Adam brothers' youngest clients, in his early twenties when Seton was begun, but not destined long to enjoy his house. According to local tradition, he had evicted an old woman who lived in a cottage near Seton Palace. She laid a curse on him and prophesied, as her house was demolished, that the new Seton Castle would never become his family home (*Burke's Landed Gentry* (1894), Mackenzie of Portmore).

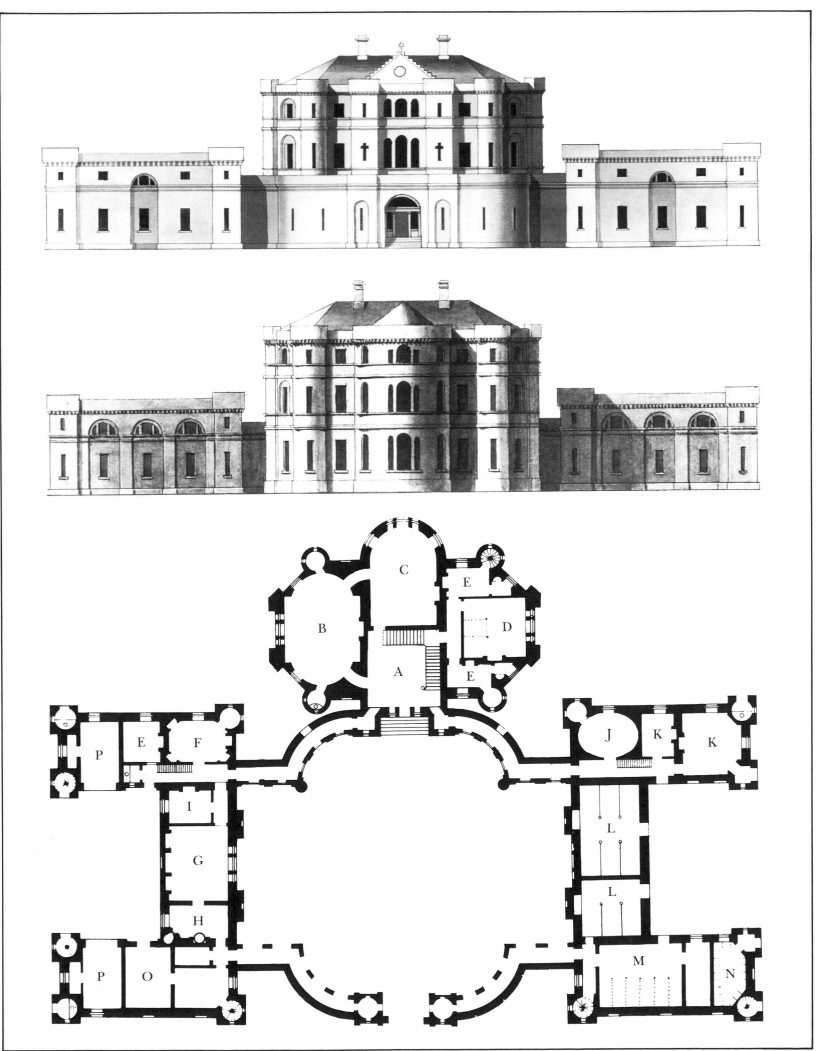

Pl. 56

Plate 57

Design for Seton Castle, Tranent, East Lothian, for Alexander Mackenzie of Portmore.

First-floor plan with a side elevation and a sectional elevation across the forecourt.

Small-scale drawing. The sectional elevation, vol. 46, no. 147. *Insc. Section through the court of Seton Castle*. The plan is taken from the office outline copy in vol. 33, no. 90 inked in for this publication. The drawing of the side elevation is modern based on vol. 33, no. 95. The use of the rooms is as follows:

A	Library	E	Kitchen continued	H	Cheese room
B	Bedrooms	F	Hay loft	I	Servants' bedrooms
C	Closet	G	Granary	J	Butler's bedroom
D	Billiard room				

The frontages extend 188 and 136 ft.
Original scale 1 in. to 25 ft.: here 10 mm. to 10 ft.

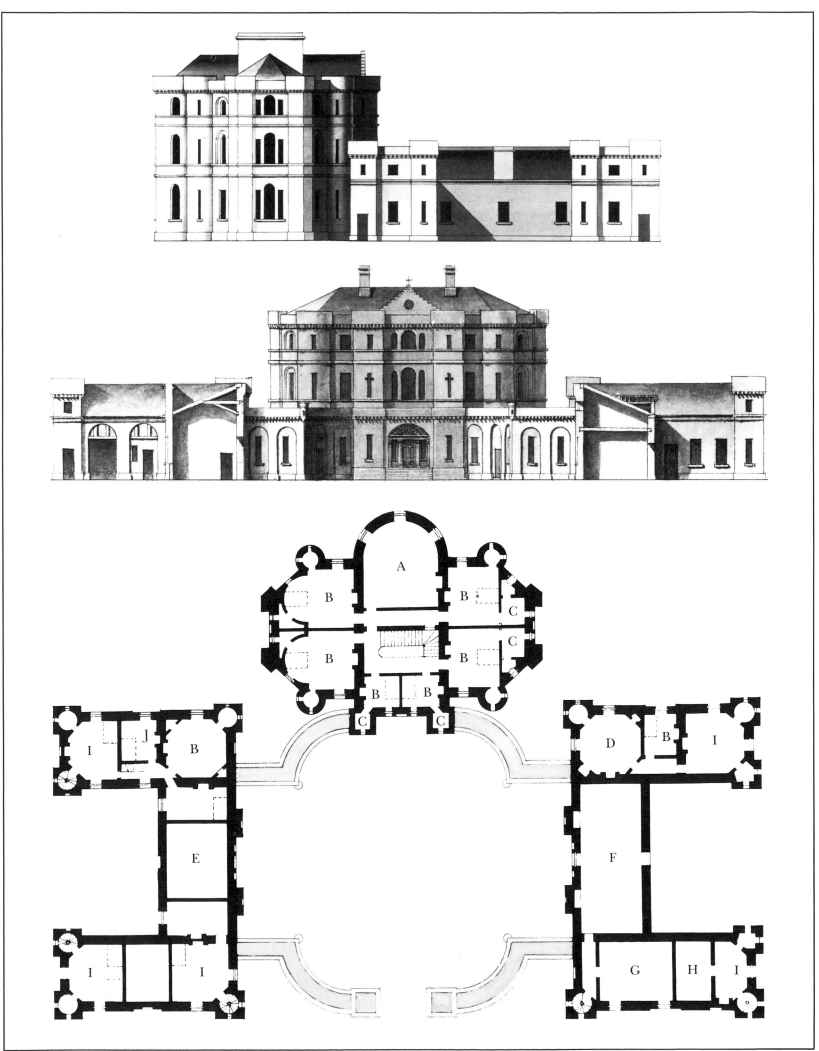

Pl. 57

Plate 58

Design for a new residence at Findlater Castle, Fordyce, Banffshire, for James Ogilvy, Earl of Findlater.

Plan of the parlour storey with the principal elevation of a palatial rectangular castle arranged round an oval staircase with castellated *porte-cochère* in the centre of the northeast front and circular corner turrets at every angle.

Small-scale drawing. None of the drawings prepared for engraving in vol. 46 records this design, though an outline pen drawing of the plan, to the same scale as some of the 'miniature' designs, is preserved in vol. 1, no. 191. The elevation is reduced from an original presentation drawing now in a private collection. The use of the rooms, as indicated on the design drawings, vol. 36, nos. 26–35, is as follows:

A	Hall	E	Lord Findlater's room	I	Bedchamber
B	Principal Stair	F	Mr. Wilson's room	J	Dressing-rooms
C	Eating-room	G	Servants' hall	K	Valet
D	Common eating-room	H	Housekeeper	L	Clerk

The frontage extends 153 ft.
Original scale 8 mm. to 10 ft.: here 8 mm. to 10 ft.

Adam's proposals for Findlater Castle require some explanation. The house is vast, over-provided with accommodation—including three dining rooms, one of which is 40 ft. in diameter—and with three staircases symmetrically disposed about an axial line. No eighteenth-century aristocrat could have required a house of such extravagant proportions, yet it would seem that in this commission Adam was working closely to his client's ideas. In the summer of 1789 he and John Clerk of Eldin had visited Lord Findlater at Cullen House, when Adam had taken instructions for this gigantic scheme, of which a primitive first draught, probably by the earl, is preserved in vol. 1, no. 205 on the back of some of notes in Adam's hand about a gardener's house at Cullen. In the same year however Adam had made a very polished design for a town mansion for Lord Findlater at Portland Place, London, and it no doubt made for good relations to visit Cullen and to appear to enter into the spirit of his client's ideas. The architect's private views are recorded in a letter of 20 October 1789 to Thomas Kennedy of Dunure, his client at Dalquharran: 'I have made a new edition of a plan for Lord Findlater but whether he will ever begin to build it I dont know; if a new edition could be made of himself I would be more able to answer your question.' Neither Findlater House in London nor the castle, which was to be built on a promontory overlooking the sea two miles from Cullen House, was ever begun.

The circumstances of this commission are curious and suggest that Lord Findlater (1750–1811) was indulging in self-deception, if not pure *folie de grandeur*. His father, the 6th Earl, was a noted agricultural improver who in 1770 took his own life. The Findlater estates were then saved from having to be sold only through the good management of the 7th Earl's mother, and it seems unlikely that in a space of twenty years the son should have accumulated sufficient funds to be able to contemplate building on such a scale. He had in any case, no need for such a house; though he married in 1779 the Earl soon ceased to live with his wife, who was replaced by a companion, Mr. Wilson, for whom accommodation is provided in Adam's plan. He had no children by his marriage and is recorded in the *Gentleman's Magazine* as living almost entirely on the Continent where he died, at Dresden, at the age of 61 (*The Scots Peerage*, vol. IV, p. 40; *Complete Peerage*, vol. 5, p. 384; a copy of Adam's letter to Kennedy of Dunure is in the N.M.R.S.).

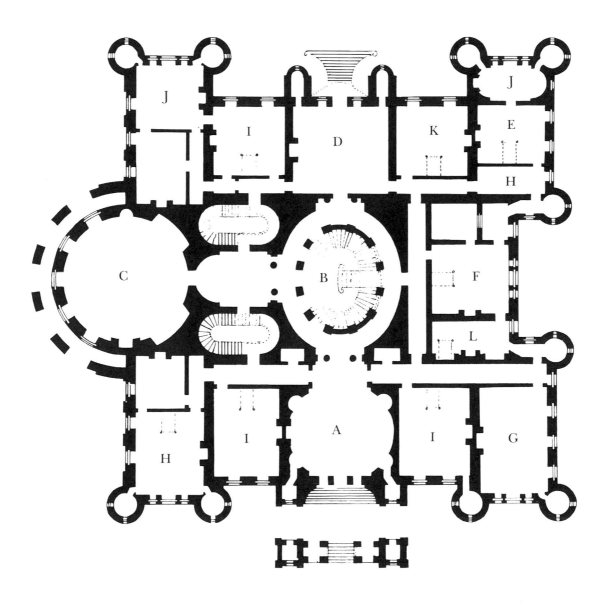

Pl. 58

Plate 59

Design for a new residence at Findlater Castle, Fordyce, Banffshire, for Earl of Findlater.

Plan of the principal floor with the southwest elevation of a palatial rectangular castle arranged round an oval staircase with a circular saloon in a round tower at the centre of the southeast front and circular corner turrets at every angle.

None of the drawings prepared for engraving in vol. 46 records this design. The elevation and plan are reproduced from the design drawings, vol. 36, nos. 26 and 34. *Insc. Principal or one pair story of Findlater Castle*. In the originals the walls in the plan and the round tower in the elevation are not finished with washes. The use of the rooms is as follows:

A	Principal staircase	F	Billiard room
B	Saloon	G	Bedchambers
C	Eating-room	H	Ante-room
D	Drawing-room	I	Dressing-rooms
E	Library	J	Lady's dressing-room

The frontage extends 159 ft.
Scale here 8 mm. to 10 ft.

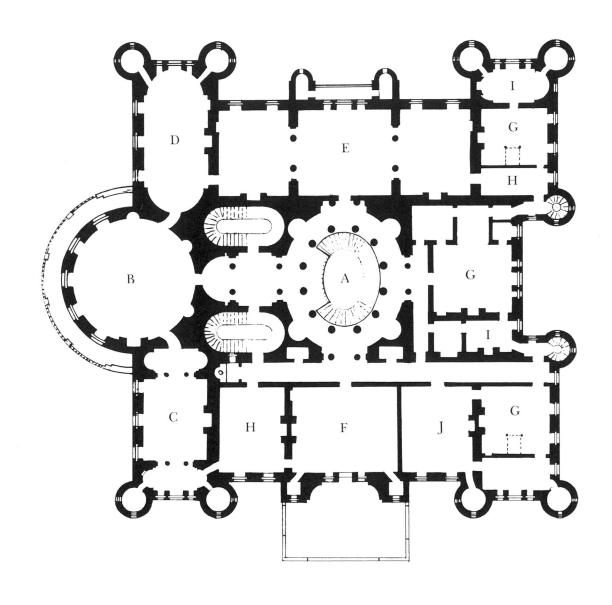

Pl. 59

Plate 60

Design for Airthrey Castle, Stirling, Stirlingshire, for Robert Haldane Esquire.

Principal elevation with the ground-floor plan of a large castle-style house and forecourt. The front, rectangular with a round tower in the centre linked to projecting corner blocks; the garden façade designed on a continuous curve, with a central square block and projecting bay.

Small-scale drawings. Three sheets of original drawings prepared for publication survive for this design, vol. 46, nos. 138–40. Two more, probably of the rear elevation, 140 × 254 mm., and of the ground-floor and courtyard plan, 198 × 300 mm., have been torn out. Their place is made up here by the design drawings, vol. 48, nos. 83 and 81. *Insc. Unknown*. The use of the rooms is as follows:

A	Hall	D	Library	G	Nursery
B	Drawing-room	E	Bedroom	H	Gentleman's dressing-room
C	Eating-room	F	Lady's dressing-room	I	Butler's pantry

The frontage extends $105\frac{1}{2}$ ft.
Original scale 1 in. to 25 ft.: here 10 mm. to 10 ft.

The commission for Airthrey Castle seems to have originated from Robert Adam's penultimate visit to Scotland in 1790, when he spent from mid-May until early October working in Edinburgh. The earliest designs for the house, a classical scheme not unlike Kirkdale (vol. 48, nos. 75–80), are dated 5 July 1790. This proposal was followed by the present castle-style design which, though none of the drawings is dated, was probably drawn up after Adam's return to London. The plan of the building relates thematically to earlier geometrical work such as the schemes for Great Saxham or Mr. Robinson's villa (Pls. 13 and 16), while its carefully constructed sequences of rooms suggest a design that was produced at leisure rather than in a bout of hectic activity which must have characterized Adam's working pattern in Scotland. On 2 March 1791 John Paterson in Edinburgh reported to Robert in London that Mr. Haldane had called to say that he was charmed with his castle and wanted to build it according to Adam's plans. Sketch proposals for the main floor plan and for both fronts are in vol. 1, nos. 27, 72 and vol. 2, no. 119. An earlier version of the design, proposing a rectangular house with curved corners rather than the D-plan shown here, is in vol. 1, no. 45.

Robert Haldane (1764–1842) proved to be a disappointing client. He had inherited the Airthrey estate when he was only four years old and at the age of sixteen had become a junior officer in the Royal Navy from which he retired in 1783. In 1786, the year of his marriage to Katherine Cochrane Oswald, Haldane settled at Airthrey and spent the next ten years in improving the estate with plantations and in excavating a large artificial lake above which the castle is placed. Adam would have enjoyed the opportunity to place a castle in this romantic situation but relations with his client became strained over Haldane's dealing directly with Thomas Russell, who had built Seton Castle and who agreed to undertake Airthrey at a lower price without any supervision from the architect. By 26 March 1791 Adam had decided to present his bill for the designs and his expenses— £37.6s.2d.—and wrote to Paterson instructing him to do so and to have nothing more to do with the commission. Airthrey Castle was in consequence executed without supervision, and the forecourt with interval towers, envisaged in these plans, was never built (*Paterson Correspondence*; Fleming 1968a, p. 1447). In 1798 Haldane, having been converted by a fundamentalist mason called Cram, who had worked at Airthrey, sold the estate to Sir Robert Abercromby and devoted the rest of his life to Protestant evangelism (R. Menzies Fergusson, *Logie, a Parish History* (Paisley, 1905), vol. II, pp. 48–53). The entrance front of Airthrey was almost completely rebuilt in a weak Scottish Baronial style about 1891 and little of the interior remains.

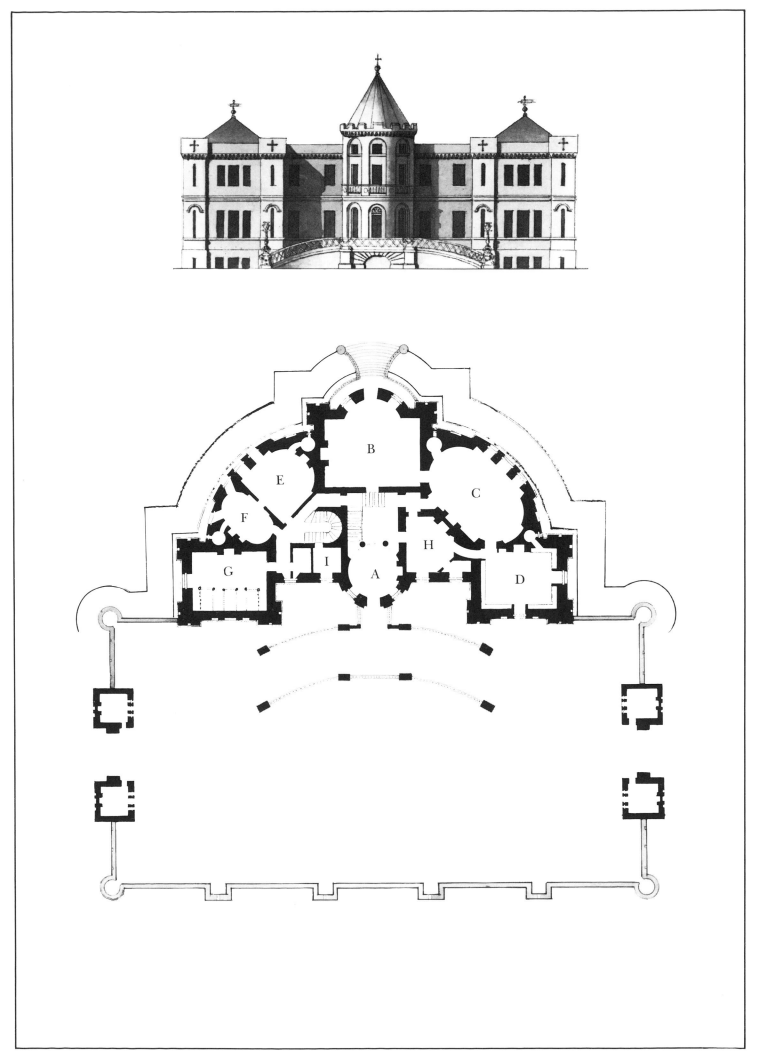

Pl. 60

Plate 61

Design for Airthrey Castle, Stirling, Stirlingshire, for Robert Haldane Esquire.

Rear elevation with the basement and first-floor plans of a large castle-style house laid out on a D-shaped plan.

Small-scale drawings. Originally two sheets. Vol. 46, nos. 139 and 140. The elevation is from vol. 48, no. 81. The use of the rooms indicated on the design drawings is as follows:

A	Servants' hall	E	Wash room	I	Bedchambers
B	Kitchen	F	Laundry	J	Dressing-rooms
C	Scullery	G	Women servants' bedrooms	K	General powdering-room
D	Men servants' bedroom	H	Housekeeper		

The frontage extends $105\frac{1}{2}$ ft.
Original scale 1 in. to 25 ft.: here 10 mm. to 10 ft.

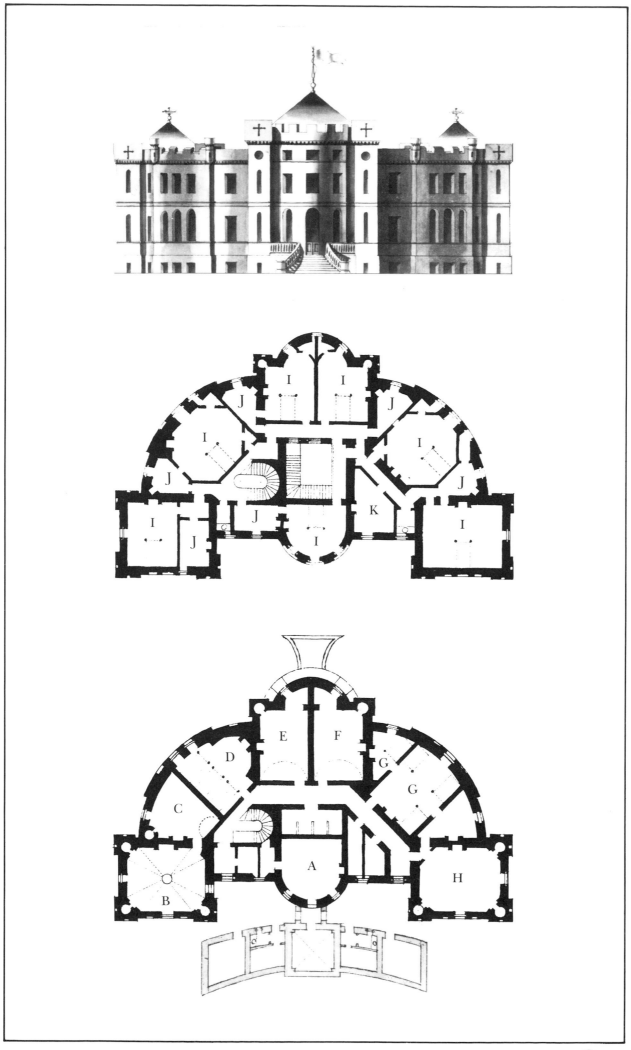

Pl. 61

Plate 62

Design for Mauldslie Castle, Carluke, Lanarkshire, for Thomas Carmichael, Earl of Hyndford.

Principal elevation with the basement and ground-floor plans of a large rectangular castle with round corner turrets and paired gable blocks on the entrance front; twin oval staircases inside and a bow on the garden front.

Small-scale drawings. Originally three sheets. Vol. 46, nos. 134–36. *Insc. Unknown*. The use of the rooms indicated on the design drawings, vol. 29, nos. 7–14, is as follows:

A	Hall	F	Library	K	Housekeeper
B	Lobby	G	Bedroom and dressing-room	L	Butler
C	Saloon	H	Kitchen	M	Maids' bedroom
D	Dining-room	I	Scullery	N	Cellars
E	Drawing-room	J	Servants' hall		

The frontage extends 108 ft.
Original scale 1 in. to 25 ft.: here 10 mm. to 10 ft.

The floor plans of Mauldslie are unique among the 'miniature' designs prepared for publication in that they have been used later in the Adam office for the practical purpose of marking the position of pipes and the flow of drains. These additions, which are casual and messy, have been removed in the drawings reproduced here. Mauldslie, probably the last castle-style composition begun in Robert Adam's lifetime, is comparatively well documented. On his last visit to Scotland in 1791 Adam made two visits to the site, one between 2 and 5 July, when the foundations of the house were probably set out, and a second on 11 September. The design drawings are signed 'Robt Adam, Architect 1791' which suggests that the plans were prepared by Adam in Edinburgh and not in the Albemarle Street office. Hugh Cairncross was responsible for superintending the construction of the castle, for which plans of the floor joists were prepared in June 1792. A courtyard of castle-style offices was designed three years later by William Adam in Albemarle Street on 22 August 1795. A sketch for the offices is in vol. 10, no. 58.

The house was built as shown in these drawings and was complete by 1796. *The Scots Magazine* described Mauldslie in September 1808 as 'built upon a plan of the late Robert Adams [sic], which is generally considered as the most complete plan of a modern castle of any designed by that celebrated architect'.

Thomas Carmichael (c. 1750–1811), 5th Earl of Hyndford, succeeded his brother William in 1778. Though the scale of the house (four reception rooms and eight principal bedrooms) suggests a large family, Lord Hyndford, like Lord Cassillis at Culzean, was a middle-aged bachelor when he began to build at Mauldslie. He remained a bachelor and was succeeded by a bachelor brother, Andrew, at whose death in 1817 the Hyndford title became extinct. The estate then passed to a nephew Archibald Nisbet of Carfin (*The Complete Peerage* vol. VII, p. 39). In 1860 a castellated *porte-cochère* and lateral wings were added to the house by James Hozier of Newlands to designs by David Bryce. The castle was demolished in 1959.

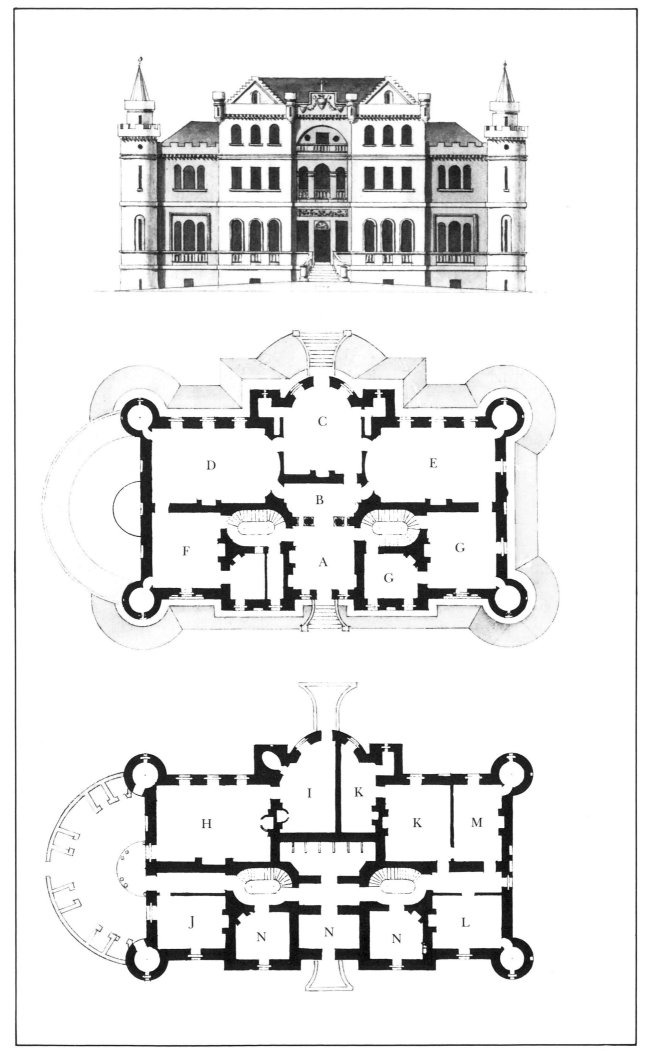

Pl. 62

Plate 63

Design for Mauldslie Castle, Carluke, Lanarkshire, for Thomas Carmichael, Earl of Hyndford.

Rear and side elevations with the first-floor plans of a large rectangular castle with round corner turrets and a bowed projection between square turrets in the centre of the garden front.

Small-scale drawings. Only the plan reproduced here is from the drawings prepared for publication. Vol. 46, no. 137. The side elevation is taken from vol. 29, no. 9, and the garden front is a modern drawing reconstructed from the design plans and a photograph of the house. The use of the rooms is as follows:

A	Bedrooms	C	Lobby
B	Dressing-rooms	D	Servants' room

The frontage extends 108 ft.
Original scale 1 in. to 25 ft.: here 10 mm. to 10 ft.

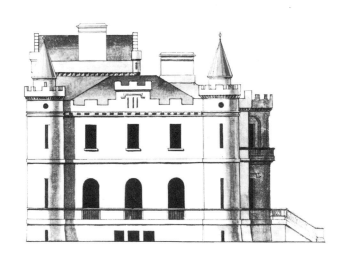

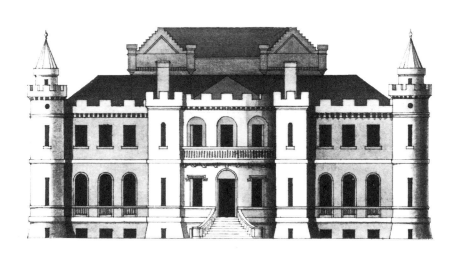

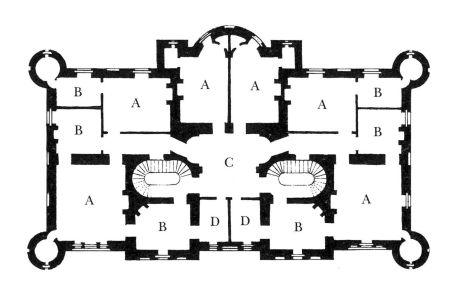

Pl. 63

Plate 64

Design for a villa in the castle style for Mr. Stevenson.

Front and rear elevation with the ground-floor and first-floor plans of a small castle. The entrance front with a projecting central block flanked by round turrets; a central polygonal tower at the back.

The front elevation trimmed to a small sheet size is in vol. 1, no. 261, and is identical in scale and presentation to the 'miniature' drawings in vol. 46. The plans are from vol. 33, nos. 76 and 77. *Insc. Principal story of a house for Mr. Stevenson.* The rear elevation is a modern drawing. The use of the rooms is as follows:

A	Hall	D	Library or dressing-room	G	Bedrooms
B	Eating-room	E	Buffet	H	Dressing-rooms
C	Drawing-room	F	Powdering-room		

The frontage extends 65 ft.
Original scales: plans $1\frac{1}{4}$ in. to 10 ft.: elevation 1 in. to 25 ft.: here 10 mm. to 10 ft.

This scheme for a small detached castle by James Adam represents the final development of the brothers' castle style. The design drawings are dated 'Albemarle Street, 26 July 1794', that is to within three months of James's death; the entrance elevation, prepared for the engraver and reproduced here, was presumably made after this date. One elevation is described as 'towards the river', from which it would appear that this commission, like the house shown on Pl. 50, may be for the Stevensons of Braidwood, Carluke, Lanarkshire.

The style of this castle is more decorative than Robert Adam's work. It lacks the robust massing of his mature designs and provides in its place a certain minute prettiness, here characterized by the small-scale battlements, the stone panelling on the turrets and the number of breaks provided on each of the main façades. The plan type, with a centrally placed top-lit stair, is typical of many Adam projects, though it may be questioned whether Robert Adam, in such a small scheme, would have proposed that the two principal rooms should be designed as identical ovals with apsed recesses in each corner. Mr. Stevenson's castle would appear to be based on a similar proposal made by James for Knockow Castle, Dunbartonshire, for John Buchanan of Ardoch who had purchased the Knockow estate in 1792. The drawings for this design (where the property is misnamed Knockear) are in vol. 30, nos. 35 and 36, and are dated 14 October 1793. Knockow Castle was to have had the same octagonal central tower with attached square turrets on the rear elevation and the same centrally placed main stair. Neither house was built, though Buchanan ultimately employed Robert Lugar to design Balloch Castle on the Knockow estate in 1809 (R. Lugar, *Plans and View of Buildings executed in England and Scotland in the Castellated and Other Styles* (1823), pls. 10–13); it was an asymmetrical neo-Norman house quite different in character to the Adam castle style. One house in Scotland that comes close to the designs for Mr. Stevenson and for Knockow is Crawford Castle near Cupar in Fife, built in 1813 to designs of David Hamilton for Lady Mary Lindsay Crawford. Hamilton, whose knowledge of the Adam brothers' late style suggests that he must at some time have worked as a clerk in their Edinburgh office, here reproduced the tripartite division of the main façade, the label mouldings, small battlements and even James Adam's personal feature of oval stone panelling on the two middle turrets of the entrance front (see J. M. Leighton, *History of Fife* (1840), vol. II, p. 243).

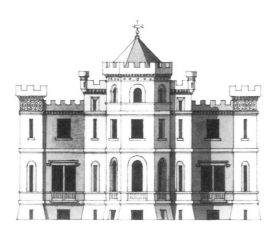

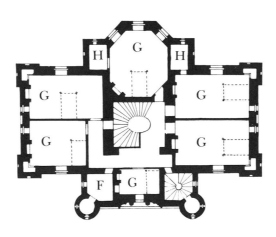

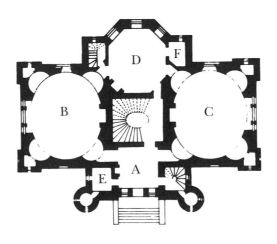

Pl. 64

The Houses as Built

For many an eighteenth-century architect there is a world of difference between the freedom of architectural design and the reality of construction. Not infrequently the author of a pattern book has been denied any opportunity to build, his conceptions have remained paper projects or, to quote Chamberlain on Wotton, 'his own castles have been in the air'. This could not be said of Robert or James Adam. In their grandest architectural essays they may traffic in the ideal, yet many of their castles, and even more of their classical villas, find a solid expression in brick or stone. The Adam designs recorded in this volume are, for the most part, real schemes. A total of forty-seven designs exists for thirty-six sites, from which no fewer than sixteen houses were built. Partly because of their location and perhaps also because they come late in the Adam story their architecture has been little studied and their appearance is not well known. Six have been demolished completely and a seventh is a roofless ruin. Of the nine that remain, five are so greatly altered that now only one classical house (Kirkdale) and three of the castles (Caldwell, Culzean and Seton) are still more or less complete. Proportionally these sixteen houses represent about half the domestic building carried out to the brothers' designs between the end of the 1770s and Robert's death in March 1792. This is perhaps a quarter, maybe even less, of the whole activity of their offices over the same period.[1]

In contrast to an earlier stage in the Adams' careers, the patrons who commissioned house designs in the 1780s and carried them into execution were men of local rather than national significance. There are no prime ministers or attorney generals, such as Bute, Shelburne or Mansfield. In England the brothers enjoyed the patronage of the romantic young Earl of Derby and the quixotic Lord Delaval; two Scottish earls, Cassillis and Hyndford, built houses to their designs yet, for the most part, their clients are drawn from a minor landed society. Four were members of parliament for a while and two of these had the reputation of being very rich. Not one client built extravagantly however and, with the possible exception of Lord Cassillis at Culzean, all were content to commission from the Adams houses appropriate to their needs.

Records survive relating to the costs of six individual houses, of which Barholm was apparently the cheapest and The Oaks the most expensive design. In the case of both these houses it is the architects' provisional estimate that is known and as there are four designs for The Oaks there are four prices for the one property. According to the design chosen, Lord Derby's castle was to cost £5,404. 5s., £5,589. 14s., £8,903. 12s. or £11,000. The house which was begun and left unfinished was built to a fifth design, in reality an elaborate remodelling of an earlier villa, for which there is no price, though an estimate based on its size suggests that it might have cost something between £6,500 and £7,000. Barholm, a modest house on a provincial estate in southwest Scotland was to cost £808. 10s., or little more than a tenth of the price of The Oaks. In this case Robert Adam's own calculations have been preserved, exhibiting a common rule-of-thumb method in which the overall dimensions of the house are established by adding together the width of the rooms and the wall thicknesses, first for the length and then for the breadth of the house, multiplying the resulting sums to calculate the area of the plan, and applying an estimated unit price per 100 square feet. Thus the plan of Barholm is calculated to be 49 by 33 feet, making a total area of 1617 square feet, which at £50 per 100 square feet works out at £808. 10s. The sketch plan that records these measurements[2] also includes quadrant wings and rectangular pavilions, though the cost of these additional buildings is not suggested in the architect's calculations. In the design that was begun (Pl. 23) the quadrants are replaced by straight links, and provision is made for a room in the basement of the main block to serve as a kitchen until such time as the wing could be built. Evidently John McCulloch, the proprietor of Barholm, was not prepared to build the entire design at once, from which we must assume that £808. 10s. represented the limit of what he could afford.

A lump price based on square measure is only a rough way by which to assess the expense of any building, and normally a more detailed estimate would have been made later. For the public buildings for which Adam had charge in Edinburgh—the university and the Calton Hill Bridewell—this was certainly done. Elsewhere it appears that the guess calculation was allowed to stand as the only estimate of cost, and an Adam building could in consequence sometimes far exceed the first price that had been quoted. In the case of the villa at Brasted Place in Kent, designed for Dr. Turton, who was a close personal friend, Adam's ideas ran so far beyond the limits of the doctor's purse that the larger scheme which was estimated to cost £11,000 had to be abandoned, or at least pruned to bring it to an agreed price of £5,500. Dr. Turton was particularly anxious to keep the price of his villa within reasonable limits, yet by 1788 when Brasted was complete even the reduced design had cost him £9,461, an increase of some 72 per cent over the original estimate, by which he was 'cruelly disappointed as well as much surprised'.[3]

By comparison with Brasted Place, the three other houses for which prices are known proved much less expensive to build. The full contract price for Seton Castle, agreed just over a year later in November 1789, was £3,400, while Airthrey Castle, begun in 1791, was to be built for £3,755. 13s.[4] Two Edinburgh brothers, Adam and Thomas Russell, took the contracts for both houses, though in the case of Seton their work was supervised by the architects while at Airthrey it was not. Unusually for an eighteenth-century building contract the Russells undertook the entire construction of these castles, tendering for each department, even to the fine joinery, paving and chimney-pieces, from which it is clear that Seton and Airthrey worked out well below the costs of Brasted Place. In the case of Mauldslie Castle, which was the last house to be begun in Robert's lifetime, a note of the time-scale for payments in his account book for 1791 gives the total contract cost for finishing the house as £4,855.[5]

What is intriguing about these costs is the manner in which they relate, or on occasion do not relate, to a standard unit price based on the floor areas of the plans. In superficial area Brasted, Airthrey and Mauldslie were all comparable designs with floor plans of 4020, 4330 and 4210 square feet. All were two-storey houses built over basements with extra accommodation in the attics. Seton too, if the two-storey wings of its courtyard are calculated as one single block, works out to a very similar floor area of 4026 square feet. So far as the three late castles are concerned there is a certain consistency. If we set Adam's lump sum price per 100 square feet at just £100, an estimated price for Seton will be £4,026, for Airthrey £4,330 and for Mauldslie £4,210. None of these sums seem very far from what we know the construction to have been, yet with Barholm and Brasted things are quite different. At Barholm Adam evidently envisaged costs at exactly half the scale of charges at Seton or Airthrey or Mauldslie (perhaps the proprietor supplied the materials himself),

while at Brasted the rate for building the house works out at well over double the cost for the Scottish castles, or £235 per 100 square feet. It may be that what we encounter here is nothing more than a Home Counties weighting. Building in or near the metropolis was always a more costly business than in the country and indeed the floor area of the various schemes for The Oaks, just like Brasted, has to be multiplied by a factor of something more than two to produce Adam's estimated costs. The problems with Dr. Turton's house may spring therefore not from any real failure to estimate accurately but more from the close friendship that existed between the architect and his client and a knowledge on Adam's part that John Turton could, as proved to be the case, pay a great deal more for his villa than the sum which he had stated to be his limit. Brasted is finished luxuriously with large slabs of very fine ashlar sandstone cramped to the structural wall. It is a construction that is handsome and aristocratic in effect but it is not one to recommend to a client whose first concern is economy.[6]

A considerable difference may be remarked in the standard of finish between the houses that were built. Two courses were open to a proprietor who employed the brothers as architects: he might buy their designs and oversee the construction himself or, as was more frequently done, he could employ the Adams as surveyors, in which case the responsibility for the proper conduct of the works rested with the architects themselves. Early in their career the brothers' charge for supervision was two and a half per cent of the contract price: by the date of the villas and castles recorded here this had risen to five per cent.[7] An Adam villa can display the closest similarity of effect between its real façades and the architecture that is recorded in the brothers' drawings. Of the designs included here, Brasted Place, Kirkdale and Jerviston (though the last has now been lost) provided noted examples of such precise correlation, yet this is not always the case. Where a client chose not to have his building supervised by the architects, or by John Paterson and Alexander Cairns, their clerks in the Edinburgh office, a wide gap might open up between what was proposed and what appeared on the ground. Glasserton and Barholm, two houses in Galloway, built at an incovenient distance from Edinburgh, the one a conversion and the other a small job, are cases in point. As they stood—both houses have now been demolished—there was a gaucheness that could only be explained by the activity of a provincial builder given too much freedom in the execution of the work. Proportions were slack, the lines of the eaves were carelessly handled and the position and shape of the windows had been adjusted in such a way as to belie entirely Adam's part in either design. That this is a matter of proportion and of the interrelationship of parts rather than of materials may be demonstrated by a comparison with Sunnyside. Like Glasserton and Barholm this house was built of rendered rubble stone. It has been badly treated in two hundred years and only a harled rear elevation survives from the original design. Except where they are dummies, all the main floor windows have been lowered, creating a haphazard effect, yet even so a certain crisp precision may be detected in the delicate cornice and blocking course at eaves level and in the square projection of its side bays. The location of Sunnyside and the close links that existed between Adam and Patrick Inglis who built the house make it clear that at this small villa the architect retained control of the construction which we may assume was not the case at Glasserton or Barholm. At Airthrey Castle in Stirlingshire, Adam was to be duped of his commission through the complicity of his client Robert Haldane and the Russell brothers who, as they had built Seton and felt they understood the Adam castle style, agreed to take the contract at a price below the architect's estimate and to cut Adam out. The remarkable bowed south front of Airthrey, which is all that can be seen of the original design today, does not suggest that the house suffered greatly by this, though Adam in correspondence with Paterson mentioned various intended improvements which were presumably left out.

In erecting these houses, the type of stonework selected clearly affected the cost, though not perhaps as much as might appear. At Airthrey the estimate prepared by the Russells if the house had been built of rubble stone was £3,500. 15s., instead of the £3,775. 13s. which was their price for executing the house in ashlar with dressed cornices. The extra cost for ashlar, which is what Haldane selected, was thus £274. 18s., or about seven and a half per cent of the whole contract price, so that, in avoiding the architect's fees for supervision, he adroitly made up the difference in cost between the rubble and the ashlar-built house. In the classical villas Adam evidently preferred that his designs should be built in smooth stonework or at least that the main façade should be of ashlar. This construction looked more precise and set off to better effect the gradations of richness on a façade, which in the understated elevations of the late villas could be limited, as at Jerviston or Kirkdale, to a shallow relieving arch and dentil cornice with the geometric precision of the masonry blocks otherwise left to speak on its own. At Walkinshaw the whole house could have been considered an exercise in pure masonry, as is the supremely austere, astylar north front of Brasted Place.

In contrast to the classical houses, the Adam castles do not seem to have required stonework of quite such precision to point up their design. Some were indeed built of polished ashlar blocks; Airthrey is a case in point, Mauldslie was another, while the impeccable masonry of Dalquharran, even as a ruin, has a keen edge that marks exactly each break in the façades. Adam's earliest castles however were usually rubble built or else finished with a rough-cast rendering contained between dressed string courses. Among the designs published here, Caldwell House offers an instance of such rendered work, where the masonry details of label mouldings, battlements, machicolated cornices and miniature bartizans breaking the roof-line, gain effect by contrast with the texture of the walls. To a modern eye it is perhaps the castles with most texture in their walls that have the best effect. The Oaks

as surviving to before World War II was only a fragment of what Adam had planned; yet the speckled texture of its round brick turrets and broad octagonal towers gave the building a congruity and air of picturesque antiquity— perhaps also a kinship with Vanbrugh castle—it could hardly have possessed if built in ashlar stone, and there can be little doubt that both Culzean and Seton gain in robustness through the varied dressing of their walls. The south front at Culzean, though it is finely built of squared sandstone blocks, is not a smooth surface but catches the light and takes life from a uniformly chanelled face on each stone which is produced by the use of a drove. The handling of the masonry on the north front above the cliff is more vigorous, while Seton, the most robust of all the castles, exploits a variety of finish, contrasting polished string courses with rubble walls, droved stone round the windows and strongly ribbed broach work on the battlements.

The synthesis of a quasi-medieval or fortified idiom with the language of classical architecture which lies at the core of the Adam castle style may be remarked in the reiterated horizontal lines of cornices and string courses in all the castles. Even the undulating rhythms of the turrets and towers in the complex form of the main block of Seton are bound together in this way. At Culzean the centre of the south front is decorated with an arcaded motif almost like a quotation from a Renaissance palazzo; the same motif is repeated on the entrance front and many of the castles make use of an incised round arch or arcade to increase the modelling of their façades. The door cases too are selected from a familiar repertoire of Adam classical designs, and it is classicism that obtains in the interiors of all the houses, whether villas or castles. By comparison with the brothers' earlier work these late houses were neither costly nor richly finished. Interior display hardly extends beyond the discreet insertion of a screen of columns in a hall or upper landing, the introduction of a delicate chimney-piece or the finishing of the public rooms with neo-classical plaster friezes which occasionally adopt a baronial iconography, as at Seton. Here the frieze in the hall alternates shallow moulds of deer heads with crossed swords on an oval shield, in a pattern recalling the arrangement of a Doric frieze. In many of the smaller designs Adam combined staircase and front hall in one lofty open space creating, if on a modest scale, at least one moment of architectural grandeur in the interior of the house. Amongst the houses that were built, this arrangement was followed at Jerviston, Barholm, Walkinshaw, Seton and, in a modified form, at Airthrey.[8] Elsewhere, a central top-lit stair was used and it is this type that provided the architect with an opportunity to create two of his most memorable stairs. At Dalquharran a clear spiral of cantilevered stone rose with exhilarating grace to a circular roof light at its apex while in Culzean essentially the same theme appears, grandly decked, in the famous central stair. Here, if nowhere else in the interiors of the late commissions, Adam achieved the heroic and the grand.

NOTES

1. The sixteen houses that were built are, Jerviston, Milburn, Brasted, Glasserton, Kirkdale, Sunnyside, Barholm, Wyreside and Walkinshaw (classical designs) and Caldwell, The Oaks, Dalquharran, Culzean, Seton, Airthrey and Mauldslie (castle-style designs). In the period from 1780 onwards Adam carried out work on ten other classical schemes at Letterfourie, Yester, Alva, Ruscombe, Newliston, Dunbar Castle, Belleville, Glencarse, Gosford and Balbardie and at six castles, Oxenfoord, Pitfour, Castle Upton, Fullerton, Stobs and Barnton. Public buildings under his direction in these years were (in Edinburgh) the Register House, the University, the Bridewell and St. George's Episcopal Chapel, and (in Glasgow) the Trades House, the Royal Infirmary, the Tron Church and the Assembly Rooms. The brothers were also involved in speculative building works in London in Portland Place and Fitzroy Square and in designs for the Edinburgh New Town, particularly Charlotte Square. For details of this work see Colvin 1978, pp. 50–55.

2. Soane Museum Adam Drawings vol. 1, no. 267. This sheet is published in Rowan 1983, p. 32. A second sheet of calculations for an unidentified classical villa is in vol. 1, no. 264.

3. In July 1788 Dr. Turton wrote to Adam to complain about the excessive cost of his house, citing the sums quoted here (Guildhall Library, London, MS. 3070). I am obliged to Professor Alan Tait for drawing my attention to this letter and for a copy of it.

4. These prices are quoted in Fleming 1968a, pp. 1444–47 and are taken in part from the *Patterson Correspondence*.

5. Sanderson 1982, p. 39.

6. Adam's failure to assess the cost of Brasted accurately need not be taken to indicate a general incompetence in this area of his business. His estimate for Airthrey was close to the sum for which the house was built, in fact a little higher, while at Brasted a comparison of the floor area of the £11,000 scheme (which was 4,900 sq. ft.) with that of the house that was built (4020 sq. ft.) will prove immediately that a 50 per cent reduction in the price, which Turton expected, was not possible.

7. Both Fleming 1968a and Sanderson 1982 quote this figure.

8. Oxenfoord and Stobs Castles also have stairs of this type.

Bibliography

ADAM, ROBERT, *Ruins of the Palace of the Emperor Diocletian, at Spalatro, in Dalmatia* (London, the author, 1764).

ADAM, ROBERT AND JAMES, *The Works in Architecture of Robert and James Adam* (London, the authors, 1773–79), 2 vols. A third volume was published posthumously in 1822. A reprint in facsimile, limited to 500 copies, was produced by E. Thézard (Dourdan, 1900). There are also reduced reprints by Tiranti (1939 and 1959), a one-volume reduced reprint of all three volumes published by Academy Editions with an Introduction by Robert Oresko (London, 1975), and a larger single-volume reprint by Dover Publications, Inc. with an introduction by Henry Hope Reed (New York, 1980).

ADAM, ROBERT, *Designs for Vases and Foliage composed from the Antique* (London, 1821); a posthumous publication without any letterpress.

ADAM, WILLIAM, *Vitruvius Scoticus* (Edinburgh, 1812); a facsimile edition with an introduction by James Simpson was published by Paul Harris (Edinburgh, 1980).

BEARD, GEOFFREY, *The Work of Robert Adam* (Edinburgh and London, John Bartholomew & Son, 1978); a commemorative essay by one of the leading historians of Georgian craftsmanship published on the 250th anniversary of Robert Adam's birth, excellently illustrated.

BOLTON, ARTHUR T., 'Robert Adam as a Bibliographer, Publisher and Designer of Libraries', *Transactions, Bibliographical Society*, vol. 14 (1915–17), pp. 22–30.

BOLTON, ARTHUR T., *The Architecture of Robert and James Adam* (London, Country Life, 1922), 2 vols. As the standard study of the Adam brothers' architecture this work includes a topographical index to the collection of Adam drawings in Sir John Soane's Museum, made and classified by Walter L. Spiers, Bolton's predecessor as curator of the Soane Museum. Spier's index has been republished separately by Chadwyck-Healey Ltd. (Cambridge and Teaneck N.J., 1979) as an accompaniment to the same company's microfilm of the Adam drawings in the museum.

BOLTON, ARTHUR T., 'The Classical and Romantic Compositions of Robert Adam', *The Architectural Review*, no. 57 (1925), pp. 28–34.

COLVIN, HOWARD M., *A Biographical Dictionary of British Architects 1600–1840* (London, John Murray, 2nd edn., 1978); contains the most authoritative modern list of works by all the members of the Adam family.

DUNBAR, JOHN G., *The Historic Architecture of Scotland* (London, Batsford, 1966); an authoritative concise survey of Scottish architecture.

FLEMING, JOHN, 'Robert Adam, the Grand Tourist', *Cornhill Magazine*, no. 1004 (1955), pp. 118–37.

FLEMING, JOHN, 'Allan Ramsay and Robert Adam in Italy', *The Connoisseur*, no. 137 (1956), pp. 79–84.

FLEMING, JOHN, 'The Journey to Spalatro', *The Architectural Review*, no. 123 (1958(a)), pp. 103–07.

FLEMING, JOHN, 'Adam Gothic', *The Connoisseur*, no. 142 (1958(b)), pp. 75–79.

FLEMING, JOHN, *Robert Adam and his Circle in Edinburgh and Rome* (London, John Murray, 1962); the classic study of the brothers' early career and background.

FLEMING, JOHN, 'Robert Adam's Castle Style', *Country Life*, vol. 143 (23 and 30 May 1968(a)), pp. 1356–59 and 1443–47.

FLEMING, JOHN, 'A "Retrospective View" by John Clerk of Eldin with some comments on Adam's Castle Style' in *Concerning Architecture: Essays presented to Nikolaus Pevsner*, John Summerson, ed. (Harmondsworth, Allen Lane Press, 1968(b)), pp. 75–84.

GIROUARD, MARK, 'Mellerstain, Berwickshire', *Country Life*, vol. 124 (1958), pp. 416–19 and 476–79.

HARRIS, EILEEN, *The Furniture of Robert Adam* (London, Alex Tiranti, 1963).

HUSSEY, CHRISTOPHER, *English Country Houses: Mid-Georgian 1760–1800* (London, Country Life, 1956).

KAUFMANN, EMIL, *Architecture in the Age of Reason* (Harvard University Press, 1955 and New York, Dover Publications Inc., 1968); a penetrating study of baroque and post-baroque architecture in England, Italy and France, 1700–c. 1820.

LEES-MILNE, JAMES, *The Age of Adam* (London, Batsford, 1947).

MACAULAY, JAMES, *The Gothic Revival 1745—1845* (Glasgow and London, Blackie, 1975); a meticulous study of neo-medieval and romantic architecture in the north of England and Scotland which includes the Adam castle style, its precursors and successors.

OPPÉ, PAUL, 'Robert Adam's Picturesque Compositions', *Burlington Magazine*, vol. 80 (1942), pp. 56—59.

ROWAN, ALISTAIR, 'Ugbrooke Park, Devon', *Country Life*, vol. 142 (20 and 27 July and 3 August, 1967(a)), pp. 138–41, 203–07, 266–70.

ROWAN, ALISTAIR, 'Paxton House, Berwickshire', *Country Life*, vol. 142 (17, 24 and 31 August 1967(b)), pp. 364–67, 422–25 and 470–73.

ROWAN, ALISTAIR, 'Wedderburn Castle, Berwickshire', *Country Life*, vol. 156 (8 August 1974(a)), pp. 354–57.

ROWAN, ALISTAIR, 'Oxenfoord Castle, Midlothian', *Country Life*, vol. 156 (15 August 1974(b)), pp. 430–33.

ROWAN, ALISTAIR, 'Robert Adam's Last Castles', *Country Life*, vol. 156 (22 August 1974(c)), pp. 494–98.

ROWAN, ALISTAIR, 'After the Adelphi: Forgotten Years in the Adam Brothers' Practice', *The Royal Society of Arts Journal*, vol. CXXII (September 1974(d)), pp. 659–710; the text of the Bossom Lectures (1974) dealing with the brothers' business affairs in William Adam & Co., the Adam castle style and the ideal villas.

ROWAN, ALISTAIR, 'Sunnyside and Rosebank: suburban villas by the Adam brothers', *AA files, Annals of the Achitectural Association School of Architecture* no. 4 (July 1983), pp. 29–39.

ROWAN, ALISTAIR, *A Catalogue of the Architectural drawings of Robert Adam in the Victoria and Albert Museum* (H.M.S.O, 1985(a)).

ROWAN, ALISTAIR, 'Lord Derby's Reconstruction of The Oaks', *Burlington Magazine*, October, 1985(b).

SANDERSON, MARGARET H. B., 'Robert Adam's last visit to Scotland, 1791', *Architectural History, Journal of the Society of Architectural Historians of Great Britain*, vol. 25 (1982), pp. 33–46.

SCOTTISH ARTS COUNCIL, *Robert Adam and Scotland, the Picturesque Drawings*, 1972; exhibition catalogue with an introduction by Alan A. Tait.

STILLMAN, DAMIE, *The Decorative Work of Robert Adam* (London, Alec Tiranti, 1966).

STILLMAN, DAMIE, 'Robert Adam and Piranesi' in *Essays in the History of Architecture presented to Rudolph Wittkower* (London, 1967), pp. 197–206.

STILLMAN, DAMIE, 'Robert Adam', in *Macmillan Encyclopedia of Architects* (New York, The Free Press, 1982), pp. 20–32.

SUMMERSON, JOHN, *Architecture in Britain: 1530–1830* (Harmondsworth, The Pelican History of Art, 1953, 6th edn., 1977).

SWARBRICK, JOHN, *Robert Adam and His Brothers* (London, Batsford, 1915).

TAIT, ALAN A., 'The Picturesque Drawings of Robert Adam', *Master Drawings*, vol. 9, (1971), pp. 161–71.

TAIT, ALAN A., 'The Sale of Robert Adam's drawings', *The Burlington Magazine*, no. 120, (July 1978), pp. 451–54.

TAIT, ALAN A., 'Robert Adam and John Clerk of Eldin', *Master Drawings*, vol. 16, No. 1 (1978), pp. 53–57.

TAIT, ALAN A., *Robert Adam at Home 1728–1978* (R.I.B.A., autumn 1978); exhibition catalogue of some drawings from Blair Adam.

TAIT, ALAN A., 'Robert Adam's Picturesque architecture', *The Burlington Magazine*, vol. 123 (July 1981), pp. 421–22.

Index